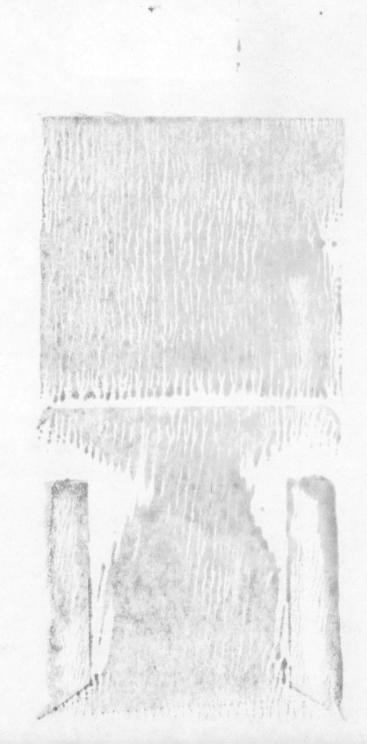

THE MODERN NATIONS IN

HISTORICAL PERSPECTIVE

ROBIN W. WINKS, *General Editor*

The volumes in this series deal with individual nations or groups of closely related nations throughout the world, summarizing the chief historical trends and influences that have contributed to each nation's present-day character, problems, and behavior. Recent data are incorporated with established historical background to achieve a fresh synthesis and original interpretation.

ROBERT O. COLLINS is Associate Professor of History at the University of California, Santa Barbara. In addition to numerous scholarly articles on the Sudan, Professor Collins is the author of *The Southern Sudan, 1883-1898* and co-author, with Peter Duignan, of *Americans in Africa*.

ROBERT L. TIGNOR is Assistant Professor in the Department of History at Princeton University. He is the author of *Modernization and British Colonial Rule in Egypt, 1882-1914,* and his articles on modern Egypt have appeared in various scholarly journals.

ALSO IN THE AFRICAN SUBSERIES

Central Africa *by Prosser Gifford*
The Congo *by Harry R. Rudin*
Ethiopia, Eritrea & the Somalilands *by William H. Lewis*
Morocco, Algeria, Tunisia *by Richard M. Brace*
Nigeria & Ghana *by John E. Flint*
Portuguese Africa *by Ronald Chilcote*
Sierra Leone and Liberia *by Christopher Fyfe*
West Africa: The Former French States *by John D. Hargreaves*

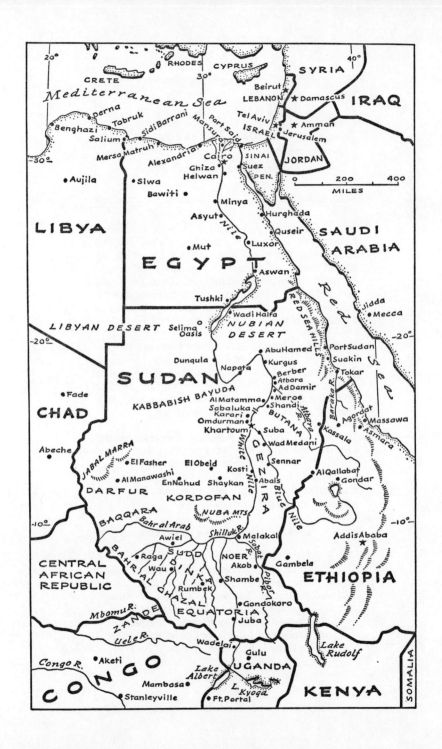

EGYPT &
THE SUDAN

Robert O. Collins
Robert L. Tignor

A SPECTRUM BOOK

Prentice-Hall, Inc.
Englewood Cliffs, New Jersey

Current printing (last number):
10   9   8   7   6   5   4   3   2   1

At the end of an age of empire both Egypt and the Sudan began a new era in which the future of the Nile Valley was at last to be fashioned not by alien conquerors but by its own inhabitants. Despite the encrustations of the past and the current interests of foreign powers, Egypt and the Sudan are determined to chart their own course within the community of nations. A greater knowledge of Egyptian and Sudanese history will facilitate an understanding of the contemporary policies and actions of these two nations. We have sought to provide a factual introduction to the modern history of Egypt beginning in the seventh century and of the Sudanese past since the great days of Kush. If we have informed where there was no prior knowledge, our purpose has been partly accomplished.

Moreover, accompanying the emergence of Egypt and the Sudan from alien rule, a large, international audience has come of age unacquainted with the two greatest nations of the Nile Valley. We cannot hope to do justice to the long and varied histories of Egypt and the Sudan, and we have purposely excluded the ancient, dynastic period except for a brief reference to the Kingdom of Kush, not so much to elucidate its historical role in the Nile Valley but to demonstrate its importance in the history of tropical Africa. Our purpose has also been to present, in addition to a factual historical outline, a readable, interpretive account of these two new nations which have arisen from the past cultures and civilizations of the Nile Valley. If we have brought some larger meaning out of a multitude of historical facts, if the stimulus to further investigation of the histories of Egypt and the Sudan has been provided, our task will have been accomplished.

The authors wish to thank Franz Rosenthal and John Mikhail for reading the sections on Egypt, and Richard Hill and Peter Holt for scrutinizing those on the Sudan. Their useful suggestions have been warmly received and incorporated. Finally, we should like to express our gratitude to all those whose instruction, guidance, and friendship have prepared and encouraged us to write this historical essay.

R.O.C.

R.L.T.

Contents

EGYPT &
THE SUDAN

ONE

LAND, PEOPLE, AND LIVELIHOOD

Egypt

Egypt's historical development has been determined by three primary elements: the Nile, the population, and the social organization of the population. Only where the Nile waters reach the land can cultivation be carried on. The truly fundamental alterations that have occurred in Egyptian history have resulted from increased irrigation of Nile waters. In recent times the size and density of Egypt's population have become serious obstacles to modernization. The organization of this population, in villages and cities, and its system of values have influenced all efforts to transform the population and to bring modernity to Egypt. The regime of President Gamal Abdel Nasser has been at work in all three of these fundamental areas. The new Aswan Dam scheme purports to be a further transformation in the control of the Nile, and although its economic gains may be wiped out by Egypt's exploding population, Egyptian leaders continue to hope the dam will create new levels of economic development and social organization. Despite efforts to limit family size, population remains Egypt's most pressing problem even as the social organization and values of the Egyptian people are undergoing modification.

Egypt is an oasis in a desert of aridity and inadequate resources. In early times the inhabitants of the Nile Valley learned to trap the floodwaters in basins prepared beside the river. This achievement permitted them to engage in settled cultivation and laid the foundations of the great Pharaonic civilizations. Although many refinements of basin irrigation were introduced over the centuries, it was essentially this ancient system that was functioning in Egypt at the time of the French invasion in 1798.

The Nile River has two major sources. The first is the Blue Nile, accounting for 60 per cent of the total Nile waters. Emerging from Lake Tana in the Ethiopian highlands, the Blue Nile flows north to its junction with the White Nile at Khartoum. The second source is the White Nile, which flows out of Lake Victoria to meander across the swamps of Lake Kioga before crashing through the narrow defile of Murchison Falls near Lake Albert. From Lake Albert the White Nile, known locally as the Bahr al-Jabal (the Mountain River) flows northward over a series of waterfalls and rapids before its course is checked in the immense swamps of the Southern Sudan. Here the channel of the river is frequently choked by the *sadd*, floating islands of vegetation which obstruct the river and from which this eerie region derives its name, the Sudd. Emerging from the swamp at Lake No, the White Nile—at this point only about 10 per cent of the Nile flood—is swelled by the waters of the Sobat and Bahr al-Ghazal rivers to an additional 20 per cent of the total floodwaters. The Bahr al-Ghazal (the Gazelle River) drains the huge basin between the Bahr al-Jabal and the Congo-Nile watershed, but like the Bahr al-Jabal it loses much of its volume in the swamps before meeting the White Nile at Lake No. The Sobat, on the other hand, rises in the Ethiopian highlands and runs unimpeded into the White Nile south of Malakal. From there the White Nile flows northward to unite with the waters of the Blue Nile at Khartoum, forming the Gezira (from *jazira*, meaning island or peninsula), the fertile, flat plain between the Blue and White Niles which has been the traditional granary of the Sudan and is now the site of the huge Sudan cotton-growing project. From Khartoum the combined waters of the two Niles continue northward for 1900 river miles to the Mediterranean, supplemented only by the seasonal river Atbara, which emerges from the Ethiopian highlands to join the Nile just 200 miles north of Khartoum.

The Blue Nile floodwaters bring immense quantities of sedimentation from the highlands of Ethiopia, much of which was deposited on the soil in Egypt when basin irrigation was in use. The annual rise of the Nile takes place from July through December; the high point is generally reached in September or October at Cairo. Under the basin system of irrigation crop yields were precariously dependent on the strength or weakness of each year's flood. If the flood was low, water would not be available for all the lands usually irrigated and cultivated. Conversely, if the flood was high, there was danger that the waters might break through the barriers along the banks of the

Nile and run uncontrolled over the land. The hydraulic improvements carried out in Egypt in the nineteenth and twentieth centuries have mitigated the effects of high and low floods quite effectively.

The rhythm of Nile flooding and the basin system of irrigation imposed a unique order on the countryside and the organization of life in Egypt. Because much of the land remained under water for a considerable time during the flooding season, people had to live in villages elevated above the rest of the land. Indeed, much land was held communally by the village group and was periodically redivided by the village elders as population changes occurred. Most of the land was watered but once and consequently supported only one harvest per year. Grains were the most common crops. Although the fertility of the Nile Valley usually assured abundant harvests, the farmer invariably was reduced to bare subsistence after his surplus had been siphoned off by the ruling elite. Most of what later became Egypt's principal cash crops—cotton and sugar especially—were summer crops, and only land near the Nile or near some source of underground water could support them. Irrigation waters were raised to the soil during the low stage by primitive techniques known to Egyptians since ancient times.

Only since the nineteenth century have steam pumps been employed to supplement and finally replace the traditional instruments for irrigating lands. The transformation of the techniques of irrigation began early in that century and continues today, the present stage being the Aswan High Dam, with the development of subsurface water in the western desert envisioned for the future. This technological revolution may be subsumed under the heading of perennial irrigation, a system under which water is provided throughout the year, whenever and wherever it is needed. Early efforts to introduce perennial irrigation were made as part of the modernizing program of Muhammad Ali (1805-48). At first deep irrigation canals were dug, capable of carrying low-stage waters to the land during the summer. Subsequently a series of dams was constructed across the Nile itself, designed to raise the level of the low stage and thus facilitate irrigation. The linchpin of the system was the Aswan Dam (completed in 1902), one of the largest hydraulic structures of its day, a remarkable feat of engineering skill which provided irrigation waters for nearly all of Egypt. To provide even greater water storage its height has twice been increased.

But the Aswan Dam will be dwarfed by the new High Dam now under construction upstream from it. The High Dam will create a lake with an area of four thousand square kilometers and a volume of 130 milliard cubic meters. It will enable new land to be cultivated and the system of perennial irrigation to be applied generally throughout Egypt. It is designed to equalize the supply of water available from one year to the next by storing the high floods for use in less abundant periods. The dam is also an integral part of Egypt's efforts to industrialize; it will provide a much needed source of electrical power.

Perennial irrigation brought immense agricultural and economic changes. Irrigation water in summer made possible the growth of cash crops. With its favorable climate and fertile Nilotic soil, Egypt is ideal for cotton cultivation, and from the beginning of the technological revolution in irrigation cotton has been the leading summer crop and principal export commodity. In fact, Egypt is the world's primary exporter of high quality, long-staple cotton fibers which are rivaled on the international market only by a few varieties of American cotton. Cotton was first exported during the reign of Muhammad Ali, but its cultivation was principally stimulated by the decline of American cotton exports during the American Civil War. Indeed, from the 1860s until the 1950s cotton accounted for nearly 80 to 85 per cent of the total value of Egyptian exports. Recent efforts have been made to diversify the economy and reduce the country's dependence on cotton exports, but cotton still assumes the major role in the economic affairs of Egypt.

Hydraulic change brought social alterations in its wake. Because the water is now brought to the land in canals and does not lie on the soil for extended periods during the flood season, the village communal system no longer has its former compelling force. Individual houses can be built anywhere on the land. New settlements have grown up all over Egypt. The village is still the basic form of social organization, for old patterns are difficult to break and as much land as possible must be cultivated, but there has been a marked dissolution of village communalism. Throughout the nineteenth century private landholding gradually replaced the communal system. By the end of the century the old legal restrictions against private landed property had been abolished, and the traditional practice of periodic reallocations of village land came to an end. The great beneficiaries of the new system proved to be the wealthy classes, most especially the royal family, who were able to amass for themselves immense tracts of land. On the other hand, the smaller peasantry were increasingly dispossessed and impoverished. They gradually became a rural proletariat working on the land of the large estate owners. The revolution of 1952, of course, had as one of its fundamental goals the confiscation of land from large landholders and its redistribution to the peasantry.

Perennial irrigation has had other drawbacks. In the interwar period medical experts conducted a survey in a village community where perennial irrigation was just being introduced. They discovered that the community, which had formerly had a low incidence of belharzia, Egypt's most widespread disease, became highly infected. This might have been predicted, for the belharzia worm must live in water snails before passing to human beings. In areas where canals remained dry part of the year, the belharzia worms died and the incidence of the disease was low. But it seems apparent that the introduction of perennial irrigation throughout Egypt has resulted in a marked increase in the disease. Belharzia affects the intestinal tract, causing the carrier to pass blood and to become phlegmatic and easily fatigued. There are no truly accurate figures, but some estimates suggest that 75 per cent of the rural population are infected with belharzia and suffer from its debilitating effects.

The Egyptian population is predominantly Muslim, although there is an important Coptic Christian minority community, and almost entirely Arabic-speaking. Arabic is a Semitic language which developed originally in the Arabian peninsula and was carried throughout the Middle East by Arab Muslim conquerors, administrators, merchants, and scholars. Despite regional variations in colloquial Arabic, the written language itself is a considerable force for unity throughout the Arab world. It also has the prestige of being the language of Islam, the language of Muhammad and the Koran, and therefore it occupies a special place in all Muslim countries.

Egypt's religious and linguistic unity tends to obscure the great diversity of its population. Actually, Egypt has been overrun by many conquerors, and most have left some influence among the population. The original population, which created the great Pharaonic civilizations of ancient Egypt, spoke a Cushitic-Semitic language, distantly related to the Berber languages of northwest Africa. Christianity came to Egypt as it spread throughout the Mediterranean basin. Its influence is seen today in the Coptic community, whose members have maintained an identity of their own and have traditionally played important roles in the Egyptian bureaucracy. The absorption of Arab and Islamic influences proceeded throughout Egypt only gradually after the Arab conquest. Then, superimposed upon these elements came later waves of Turkish-speaking conquerors. Other Middle Eastern groups, Lebanese and Syrians, came to Egypt as merchants, and finally in recent times there have been large numbers of Europeans in the country, although most were not permanent settlers.

Undeniably the single most significant force inhibiting Egyptian modernization is the rapid pace of population increase. The census of 1960 calculated the population at twenty-six million, making Egypt far and away the leader in population in the Arab East and North Africa. Population density in proportion to arable (not total) land surface places Egypt in the highest category, with heavily industrialized states like Belgium. But, of course, Egypt is not yet industrialized, and the overwhelming majority of the population still lives in the agrarian sector. Farming must thus be carried on in the most intensive fashion, but with manpower in the place of machines. The crop yields per acre are very high, among the highest in the world, but the crop yields per unit of manpower are exceedingly low because of Egypt's great semiemployed and unemployed rural labor force.

Egypt's population problem is quite a remarkable phenomenon. When the French invaded in 1798, they found a country quite sparsely populated. Their statistics must be viewed with caution, but they do seem to provide useful guides. The French scholars estimated the total population of Egypt to be around two and one-half million. Throughout the nineteenth century population pressure was not recognized as a problem in Egypt. Indeed, Lord Cromer, Britain's proconsul in Egypt from 1883 to 1907, argued that Egypt, unlike India, had no surplus of population. The first warning was not sounded until a British scholar in Egypt, J. I. Craig, published an article in an Egyptian periodical in 1917.

If the rate of increase elicited at the last census is maintained, it is not difficult to show that, in 50 years time, the population will be about 29 millions. The cultivable land will then be 7.7 millions of feddans cropped twice a year and so equivalent to 15.4 million feddans of land. . . . Now 4.4 million feddans at present barely support

13.1 million of people; will 8.7 [sic] million feddans support the 29 million of 1967? Yes if the yield of crops is improved; no if it is not.[1]

This rapid growth of population can be charted, without great precision to be sure, but in a rough fashion. The potential for growth has always been present in Egypt, for like other nonmodernized societies the country has had high birth rates. The application of modern technology has reduced death rates, but the birth rates have remained high. Until the end of the Second World War medical science was probably not the primary cause of the decreasing death rates, for advanced Western medical technology could not be brought to the majority of the people because it was expensive and clashed with many traditional practices. The one truly important exception to this statement was the control and, in some cases, the eradication of certain epidemic diseases. The two most virulent were cholera and plague, both of which had been imported into Egypt from other infected areas. Cholera was especially destructive, for it was a water-borne disease and could be carried all over the country through irrigation canals. With the increased knowledge of the causes of these diseases in the late nineteenth century, Egyptian officials were better able to protect the country from outside infection and to curb nationwide epidemics once a local outbreak had been reported. Indeed, Egypt has had only minor outbreaks of these diseases in the twentieth century, and this has undoubtedly been a factor in declining death rates.

More important than medical science, however, have been hydraulic, agricultural, and transportation improvements. These developments have permitted more food to be raised, a larger population to be supported on the land, and a better distribution of food products through the country. General famines have been eradicated, although the enormous population presses constantly upon the country's resources. Probably the last serious famine was during the troubled times from 1879 to 1882, just prior to the British occupation. Railroads have made it possible to eradicate even local famines. To be sure, there is great malnutrition in Egypt, especially among the infant population. There have been periods of near famine, but there has been nothing to resemble the frequent and severe famines

[1] J. I. Craig, "The Census of Egypt," *Egypte Contemporaine*, 1917, quoted in Charles Issawi, *Egypt in Revolution: An Economic Analysis* (New York: 1963), p. 33.

which occurred before the end of the nineteenth century. At least until 1945, increased economic productivity most generally accounted for the rising population. Since then the widespread use of antibiotics and insecticides have produced another significant reduction in death rates.

The configuration of Egypt's population presents some interesting features. If one were to accept the figure of twenty thousand in any small area as constituting an urban conglomeration, then nearly 36 per cent of the population would be urban. This is misleading, for many of the large population clusters are only sprawling village settlements and should not be classified as urban areas. Since the enormous population is squeezed into a small amount of land along the banks of the Nile, rural settlements have surprisingly more than twenty thousand inhabitants. In reality, most of the authentic urban population is to be found in Egypt's two great cities, Cairo (3,346,000) and Alexandria (1,513,000). Together they contain 60 per cent of the trading firms, 72 per cent of the brokerage firms, 52 per cent of the warehouse companies, and 45 per cent of the banking establishments. Although Egypt is fortunate to possess two such immense cities, they are actually obstacles to more widespread urbanization. They are so large as to be quite distinct, even alien, from the rest of Egypt. They do not help to transmit urban values into the rural environment. Intermediate size cities, which might perform this role, are lacking, for the surplus rural population seems to migrate only to these two major urban centers.[2]

What are the prospects for the Egyptian population problem? Unhappily, scholars appear to agree that population growth has not yet begun to slacken and will erase attempts to modernize and raise the standard of living. The impressive economic gains expected after completion of the High Dam will be swallowed up by an expanding population. The government seems to be aware of this, but its efforts have not yet matched its recognition of the problem. Immense obstacles do, in fact, exist: the ignorance and traditions of the people and the opposition of more conservative segments of the society. So far the government's programs of birth control and family planning have been limited and not particularly effective in controlling birth rates.

[2] Janet Abu-Lughod, "Urbanization in Egypt: Present State and Future Prospects," *Economic Development and Cultural Change*, XIII, No. 3 (April 1965), 313-43.

In Egypt there are three major forms of social organization: beduin, village, and urban. The bediun has always been an essential part of Middle Eastern life. He lives on the less productive land, usually as a nomad. Despite his periodic raids against settled communities he has an integral place in the economy, trading the products of his endeavors, mostly animal products, in return for the agricultural and industrial products of settled societies.

The beduin strongholds have always been in Upper Egypt, where they once enjoyed a relative autonomy from the central government of Cairo. They often led rebellions against the government, and it was to these beduin areas that ousted political factions frequently fled for safety. In the twentieth century, however, the airplane and the automobile have enabled the central government to exercise increasing control over the beduins. Moreover, throughout Egyptian history there has always been a steady trickle of beduins coming to settle on the land, for the attraction of the more stable agricultural life has been compelling, especially during bad economic times. This rate of settlement has accelerated in modern times, and presently Egypt has only a small but hardy beduin element.

The basic unit of beduin organization is the clan within the tribe, and any individual who does not belong to a clan is virtually without identity. The beduin clan serves both economic welfare and political security. The beduin code of ethics stresses honor, hospitality, and commitment to one's relatives in the clan. Crimes against members of a clan are characteristically settled by revenge. The beduin is contemptuous of the village dweller, and during hard times only the lesser members of the tribes are forced to become farmers.

Most Egyptians live in village communities where the fundamental social unit is the extended family. The family was long the most significant institution in Egypt and performed many of society's essential functions. In addition to functions commonly associated with modern Western families, the Egyptian family provided much of the education for its younger members, was fundamental in settling judicial disputes, and served as a source of political power in the community and an arbiter in assigning economic roles and resources. For instance, the economic function of a member of the family was allocated on the basis of a person's age and relationship within the family.

The socialization of the young within this extended family environment formed the basic personality type of the village community. Although an infant was one of the family's supreme blessings, and consequently denied almost nothing during the first years of his life, the permissiveness of early life was succeeded by increasing parental supervision and discipline. Parents demonstrated little understanding of the child's world, its fantasies and games. The child was expected to be exceedingly respectful of his parents, to master their values, and to be useful to his parents in daily chores. This type of upbringing produced adults who were productive, persistent, oriented to the practical and concrete, rigid in outlook, and conformist. Their fantasy world was repressed, and they made little use of creative imagination.

The most severe of the disciplines in the socialization of the young were associated with sexuality. From puberty the sexes were strictly segregated. Chastity was extolled as the highest virtue of the young. Great shame and apprehension were associated with sex. As one observer put it: "This excessive prohibition on sexuality at the stage of adolescence was a social discipline imposed to create and perpetuate the attitude of timidity and dependence of the growing individuals on their seniors. To obey such a discipline was a method of ingratiation and of establishing conditions for being loved, protected, and socially accepted. Thus it worked as a lever which parental authority manipulated to make children acquiescent and dependent and as a social technique for minimizing initiative and ambition. These exaggerated cravings of dependency and their concomitant consequences of the inflation of the parental image and social conformity probably explain the psychological undercurrents lying behind the great indifference to social change in this village as well as in many other similar communities in Egypt." [3] Individuals reared this way were responsive to external standards. They displayed great concern over personal honor and reputation, especially in matters of land and family.

The new urban environment has been the real cauldron of social change and personality transformation. Egyptians have been attracted to cities because of their greater educational and economic opportunities or because of rural dislocation. The westernized or modernized institutions of Egypt are mainly located in the larger cities: modern schools, government bureaucracy, new industries, commerce, and the army. It is from men trained in these schools and engaged in

[3] Hamed Ammar, *Growing up in an Egyptian Village; Silwa, Province of Aswan* (London: 1954), p. 191.

the new professions that Egypt's present elite is drawn. In contrast to village dwellers and often in contrast to the old ruling elites, its members are more open, imaginative, creative, not so excessively concerned with personal honor and reputation, and less tied to the rules handed down from the past.

The Sudan

On New Year's Day, 1956, the flags of Great Britain and Egypt were hauled down all over the Anglo-Egyptian Sudan, and the blue, yellow, and green flag of the Republic of the Sudan was raised in their place. Thus ended the Condominium, fifty-seven years of British and Egyptian rule in the Sudan, which began after the collapse of the authoritarian Mahdist state on the battlefield of Karari in 1898 and closed with the inauguration of an independent, democratic Sudan in 1956. Dominated by the British, the Condominium is the decisive epoch in modern Sudanese history, that era in which the introduction of Western ideas and institutions by British officials combined with the less conspicuous revival of Egyptian cultural influence to change forever the traditional patterns of Sudanese government and society. Egyptian (or in the early years Turko-Albanian) ascendancy had come to the Sudan in the nineteenth century with the armies of Muhammad Ali, only to be eclipsed after 1881 by the meteoric rise of the Mahdist state. Later, Egyptian cultural influence returned with the Anglo-Egyptian armies and remains undiminished to this day. The British impact was even greater. They sought to modernize the Sudan by applying technology to the subsistence economy on the one hand, while grafting the liberal institutions of England to the authoritarian, traditional society of the Sudan on the other. Although British officials brought the technology of Europe and the parliamentary democracy of England to the Sudan, they themselves were ironically neither democrats nor scientists but administrators who believed that their political traditions and imperial heritage invested them with a unique ability to rule and who assumed that the triumphs of Western technology endowed them with a cultural supremacy. Sure of their institutions, convinced of their cultural superiority, their ideas and institutions dramatically altered the customary Sudanese relationships of tribe, religion, and home, creating conflicts and tensions which compromised even the most ordinary, everyday tasks and disrupted even the most accepted customs. Here then, within this cauldron of modernization, lies the substance of the modern history of the Sudan, a product of the interaction of two cultural reagents, Britain and Egypt, with indigenous Sudanese society.

The Republic of the Sudan is a vast land of nearly a million square miles and some twelve million inhabitants. It stretches southward from the second cataract of the Nile at 22° North latitude to Lake Albert near the equator. The population is overwhelmingly rural, but an urban complex, consisting of the three cities of Khartoum, Omdurman, and Khartoum North, is rapidly emerging at the juncture of the Blue Nile and the White Nile. Khartoum was founded on the site of a small village in 1824 as the headquarters of the Egyptian army in the Sudan. An administrative center in a strategic geographical position, Khartoum developed rapidly until destroyed and deserted by the Mahdists in 1885. After the defeat of the Mahdists in 1898, Khartoum was rebuilt by the British as the capital of the Sudan and remains today the administrative center of approximately 100,000 inhabitants and the bastion of Western influence, symbolized by the University of Khartoum, the European shops, and the recent introduction of light industry. Across the White Nile is Omdurman. Originally little more than a ferry crossing, Omdurman became the Mahdist capital after the destruction of Khartoum, and since that time it has grown into a sprawling Sudanese city with 120,000 inhabitants. Across the Blue Nile from Khartoum is Khartoum North. With a population over forty thousand, Khartoum North is more a residential and industrial suburb of Khartoum than an autonomous city. Beyond this growing urban center, numerous towns are scattered throughout the provinces, generally as administrative headquarters or, as in the case of Port Sudan and Wad Medani (each about fifty thousand), the result of economic development. Although the center of governmental, intellectual, and economic life, the cities and towns are the habitation of only a small minority of Sudanese.

Originally, *Sudan* meant *Bilād as-Sūdān*, the "land of the blacks" of the medieval Muslim geographers, which extended across Africa from the Red Sea to the Atlantic, between Arab and African cultures. The generic name *Sudan* is still applied to this extensive region, but as used in the following pages it specifically refers to those territories in the basin of the Nile which now constitute the Republic of the Sudan. Opening northward to the expansive wastes of the Libyan and Nubian deserts, the Sudan is confined in the central and southern provinces by the Red Sea and Ethiopia to the east, the Great Lakes of Central Africa to the south, and the massif of Jabal Marra to the west. The rivers and streams of the Sudan, almost all of them part of the Nile River system, play a preponderant role in Sudanese life, while the amount of rainfall governs conditions in the enormous areas beyond the reach of the rivers.

The Nile, of course, is the dominant physical feature of the Sudan. The annual flood of the main Nile reaches its peak below Khartoum in late August and early September, when it expands to sixteen times the volume of its lowest stage in April. Between mid-July and mid-September over half the total volume for the year passes through the Sudan to Egypt and the sea. North of Khartoum irrigation is essential for cultivation. Here, scattered along the Nile between Shandi and Dunqula, are some twenty depressions which are annually flooded and drained to provide crops and grazing land, but an even larger number of feddans (one feddan equals 1.038 acres) are irrigated by lifting the water from the Nile to the fields above. Traditionally, the *shaduf* (counterbalance dipper) and the *saqia* (water wheel) were employed for this purpose, but since the Second World War the use of mechanical pumps has permitted a rapid expansion of Nilotic irrigation. South of Khartoum rainfall increases, but remains so variable that irrigation is desirable. The Gezira Irrigation Scheme, for instance, is completely dependent on the water stored behind the Sennar Dam, which flows by gravity through a network of canals to be drawn off when required into fields of cotton and food crops. In the eastern Sudan two rivers, the Gash and the Baraka, which are not in the Nile system, provide water for flush irrigation. Rising in the highlands of Eritrea, the rivers rush down to the plains during the rains in a series of spates to disappear into deltas, the Gash and the Tokar respectively, upon which irrigated crops are grown.

Rainfall largely determines the way of life and the physical characteristics of the land beyond the Nile and its tributaries. In the extreme north along the present Egyptian-Sudanese frontier there is almost no rainfall, and only about one inch annually at Marawi, two hundred miles to the south. The only cultivation possible is that which can be irrigated by the tribes settled along the river banks. These peoples claim different origins. In the north along the Aswan Reach dwell the Nubians (the Sukkut and the Mahas), Muslims who still speak Nubian dialects which have given way but grudgingly to Arabic. Farther south along the Nile lives a larger group of peoples who, although having intermarried with the indigenous Nubians, describe themselves as Arabs and claim descent from a common Arab ancestor, Ibrahim Jaal. Although the historical accuracy of such ancestry is doubtful, these Sudanese people, called collectively the Jaali, take great pride in their common pedigree. Two groups in particular among the numerous Jaali tribes, the Danaqla and the Jaaliyin, have played important roles in the history of the Sudan. Located in the historic region of Dunqula, whence they derive their name, the Danaqla (men of Dunqula) have the strongest Nubian element of any of the Jaali tribes. Beyond between the Atbara and the Sabaluka Gorge live the Jaaliyin (plural of *Jaali*), who have adopted the Jaali appellation as their own tribal name. In modern times all of these tribes have felt the pressure of increased population on their lands, so that many have emigrated—the Nubians to Egypt as servants, the Danaqla and the Jaali to Kordofan and the Southern Sudan as merchants and traders. Those who have remained behind continue the rhythmic life of settled villagers governed by the rise and fall of the Nile whose waters maintain their crops, flocks, and herds.

Along this extensive reach of the Nile from lower Nubia to Sabaluka, only one tribe, the Shayqiyya, does not claim a Jaali descent. More aggressive and restless than their neighbors, the Shayqiyya alone of the riverine tribes resisted the invading forces of Muhammad Ali in 1821, were defeated, and then enlisted in the Turko-Egyptian army as irregular cavalry. During their Egyptian service they established colonies all over the Sudan, and today the Shayqiyya are among the most vigorous and adaptable of Sudanese peoples.

East and west of the Nile dwell the nomadic Arab tribes known as the *Juhayna*, a general term embracing those Arab tribes who do not claim Jaali origins. To the west of the Nile live the Kababish, who roam deep into Kordofan and Darfur with their camels and sheep and who once controlled the *Darb al-Arbain* (the Forty Days Road), the great caravan route from the western Sudan to Asyut in Egypt. To the east of the Nile between the Atbara and the Blue Nile rainfall is sufficient to provide seasonal grass. The area is known as the Butana and is dominated by the camel-owning, nomadic Shukriyya. Just as the existence of the villagers is governed by the rise and fall of the Nile, the life of these camel people is regulated by the annual cycle of the dry and rainy seasons. The Kababish, for instance, wander southward in the dry season in search of grazing and then reverse their direction in the rainy season, moving north and west to the fresh grass and the pools left by the rains. The Shukriyya remain close to the Blue Nile during the dry season but then pursue the rains north and east into the interior of the Butana. Southward from the latitude of Khartoum the rains permit limited cultivation and extensive grazing on the grasslands which stretch west from the Nile across southern Kordofan and Darfur. These plains are inhabited by tribes, known as the Baqqara, or cattle-owning Arabs, claiming Juhayna origins but influenced culturally and physically by intermarriage with Negroid peoples from the south and west. Excellent horsemen, fanatical fighters, and emotional in their religion, the Baqqara nomads, chief among whom are the Rizayqat and Taaisha tribes, conform, like the camel-owning tribes, to the cycle of seasons, moving south in the dry weather and north to higher ground with the rains. One other important Arab subgroup, the Rufaa, have in the past frequently been included among the Juhayna Arabs, but, like the Shayqiyya among the Jaali, the Rufaa possess unique origins which distinguish them from the other Juhayna tribes. Originally a nomadic people who grazed their herds and flocks on either side of the Blue Nile, all except the southern section upstream near the Ethiopian foothills have today adopted a settled, riverine existence.

Interspersed among the Arab tribes are numerous islands of non-Arab peoples, indigenes who have preserved their own cultures from the tides of Arab migrants who have passed them by or surrounded them. Far to the east in the Red Sea Hills are the largest non-Arab group in the Northern Sudan, the Beja, camel-owning Muslims who, except for the Ababda, speak their own Cushitic language. The Ababda are the most Arabized of the Beja; they speak Arabic and live partly in Egypt, and at one time they controlled the caravan route from Kurusku across the Nubian Desert to Abu Hamad. The more southern Beja tribes, the Hadendowa, Bisharin, and Bani Amir, are much less affected by Arab influences, having remained in the mountain vastness of the Red Sea Hills until the eighteenth century, when they expanded down onto the plains of the Atbara and the Gash rivers. West of the Nile in the Nuba Mountains a group of indigenous, non-Arabic-speaking, pagan, Negroid peoples have been isolated in the hilltop villages by the Arabs who seized the plains below. The Arabic language makes no distinction between the Nuba of Kordofan and the Nubians near the Egyptian frontier, resulting in a long-standing controversy on the possible relationship between the two. In the far west a third important non-Arab people, the Fur, dwell in the protection of Jabal Marra. Here the Fur maintained their identity against the conquering Arabs and preserved their own dynastic Muslim state in Darfur (land of the Fur) until 1916.

The southern limit of the Baqqara is the Bahr al-Arab, a tributary of the Bahr al-Ghazal flowing west to east and forming a natural frontier between the Arab, Muslim North and the Negroid, pagan South. Between the Bahr al-Arab and the Great Lakes of Central Africa is the land known as the Southern Sudan, whose four million inhabitants differ dramatically from the Northern Sudanese.

Ethnically the North claims to be Arab, the South is Negroid. In religion the North is Muslim, the South is predominately pagan with a sprinkling of Christians and Muslims. The North speaks Arabic, the South some eighty different languages. Culturally the North is linked to Egypt and the wider Arab world, the South to Africa and the cultures of the peoples of the Congo, Uganda, and Kenya.

Although today the leaders of the Sudan are striving to bind the disparate peoples of the North and the South with the cords of Sudanese nationalism, they are confronted by this wide cultural divergence and haunted by Southern hostility left over from historic conflicts and from the exploitation of the South by the Arab North. Moreover, the Southern Sudanese themselves cannot claim any cultural homogeneity such as Arabic or Islam, which have played such a vital role in binding together the Northern Sudan, and the internal rivalries and cultural differences within the South have greatly contributed to the failure of the Southern Sudanese today and in the past to act in common against any real or imaginary threat from the North. The many and complex institutions and cultures in the Southern Sudan defy brief description, but generally the Southern Sudanese have been divided into three great linguistic subfamilies: Eastern Sudanic, Central Sudanic, and Adamawa-Eastern.[4]

Eastern Sudanic is a subfamily of the Chari-Nile branch of the larger Nilo-Saharan language family. It contains some ten branches,

[4] I have employed the African linguistic classification of Professor Joseph H. Greenberg, "The Languages of Africa," *International Journal of American Linguistics*, XXIX, No. 1 (Jan. 1963).

three of which are represented in the Southern Sudan. Along the
Nile corridor the Nilotic branch of Eastern Sudanic is dominated
by three large and powerful tribes: the Nuer, the Dinka, and the
Shilluk. The Nuer live in the most inaccessible areas of the great
swamps of the Nile and until the most recent times have been left
alone by conqueror and administrator alike. Interested solely in his
cattle, the Nuer remains a rugged individual in a world where that
term has become an anachronism. The Dinka, numbering nearly a
million, are the single largest tribal group in the Sudan today. Like
the Nuer, their single-minded concern for cattle dominates their
economic, social, religious, and aesthetic life; all activities revolve
around the cattle camp and the seasonal migrations from the marsh
lowlands in the dry season to the high ground in the wet. The
Shilluk inhabit the west bank of the Nile north and south of Fashoda,
but unlike the Nuer and the Dinka, the Shilluk keep only a few
cattle and cultivate the land, for which their neighbors despise them.
Perhaps it is their settled way of life or the fact that Shilluk land is
concentrated near the river that accounts for the distinctive Shilluk
institutions of political organization revolving around the *Reth* or
Divine King. The Nuer, the Dinka, and the Shilluk are the principal
but by no means the only Nilotic-speaking peoples in the Southern
Sudan. At the foot of the Ethiopian escarpment live the Anuak,
who depend on sheep and goats rather than cattle for subsistence.
On the western fringe of the Dinka are small groups of Nilotic-
speaking cultivators (the Jur, Luo, Bor, Dembo), while south of the
Dinka are the Bari and related tribes (the Fajelu, Kakwa, Nyangbara,
Mandari, and Kuku) who in the depredations of the nineteenth
century lost their large cattle herds and were reduced to agriculture.
Beyond, in the mountains to the south and east on the Uganda
border, dwell isolated clusters of Nilotic-speaking peoples (the
Latuka, the Dongotoro, the Lokoya, and the Lango), offshoots of
early migrants who have remained independent, settled farmers.

Scattered on the fringe of the great funnel of Nilotic-speaking
peoples clustered along the Bahr al-Jabal and its tributaries are two
additional branches of the Eastern Sudanic subfamily. East of the
Nile live the Murle, the Longarim, and the Didinga group, while
west of the Nile on the plains of the Bahr al-Ghazal are pockets of
the Njangulgule and the Shatt, who form the third group of Eastern-
Sudanic-speaking peoples in the Southern Sudan. None display the
passion for cattle of their Nilotic neighbors, preferring a subsistence

economy based primarily on cultivation with only small numbers of livestock.

The Central Sudanic languages, like the Eastern Sudanic, are a subfamily of the Chari-Nile branch of the Nilo-Saharan language family. The vast majority of African peoples speaking languages of the Central Sudanic subfamily lie outside the basin of the Upper Nile and are represented in the Southern Sudan by only three small, weak tribes—the Kreisch, the Moru, and the Bongo.

The third language group, the Adamawa-Eastern, is a subfamily of the Niger-Congo branch of the larger Congo-Kordofanian family. The numerous subfamilies of Niger-Congo, of which Adamawa-Eastern is only one, also include the large number of related Bantu languages. Like Central Sudanic, the vast number of linguistic groups included in the Adamawa-Eastern subfamily inhabit territory outside the Sudan, but the eastward encroachment of these African peoples has left a large block of Azande-speaking people on the Sudan side of the Congo-Nile watershed. Unlike the Nilotes, they are tillers of the soil, disciplined to a central authority, and organized for expansion. During the nineteenth century the Azande and related peoples pressed north and east into the Southern Sudan, pushing back the smaller, weaker Central-Sudanic-speaking tribes onto the Nilotes and, by the end of the century, actually coming into contact with the Nilotic fringe.

The differences between the Northern and Southern Sudan are not only confined to the race, religion, language, and culture of their inhabitants, but to their land as well. The luxuriant, verdant grasslands, swamps, and forests of the South form a striking contrast to the arid plains and rocky outcrops of the North. Physically the Southern Sudan is an undulating plain rising from the swamps of the Nile south and west to the Congo-Nile Divide and the Uganda frontier, where the vegetation is green and lush and the configuration of the land is broken by ridges and low mountains. Some of the mountains, the most famous of which is Jabal Rejaf, emerge conical-shaped from the surrounding plain, presenting the illusion of great height, while others, like the Imatong Mountains on the Uganda frontier, are but one of a chain of mountain ranges, some of which tower to a height of ten thousand feet. To the west along the Congo-Nile Divide the rising plain culminates in long, parallel ridges separated by steep ravines from which rise the rivers and streams of the Nile. Near the Divide the grasslands of the Bahr al-Ghazal are interspersed with gallery forests, named for the effect of interlocking branches high above the ground. Gradually these forests thicken and then elide to form the great tropical rainforest that stretches far into the Congo.

Thus the Sudan is a vast and disparate land. Many Sudanese and non-Sudanese alike regard its diversity as a hopeless obstacle to the creation of a modern nation-state. Differences do not, however, always weaken and divide. Dissimilar cultures and divergent resources, as some nations have learned, can be fused into a unique synthesis even more viable than either of the separate parts alone. The task of the Sudanese today is to submerge their differences in the process of modernization from which a new, stronger, and more prosperous society will emerge.

TWO

EGYPT AND THE SUDAN

BEFORE THE MODERN PERIOD

Egypt Before the French Invasion

No country in the world has so illustrious, complex, and rich a history as Egypt. Some of man's earliest advances in civilization were born in the valley of the Nile. Like Babylon, Egypt has been considered a cradle of settled and organized human culture, developed and refined during the age of the Pharaohs. Later, Egypt was a province of the great empires of antiquity—Greece, Rome, Persia, and Byzantium. This short essay cannot deal with the early phases of Egyptian history. Since the seventh century and the Muslim conquest, Egypt's destiny has been inextricably linked with the Islamic world. It has been a major Muslim province and state, but even in this larger cultural system it has continued to demonstrate the rich variety of its own historical experience.

Although Islam originated in the tribal society of the Arabian peninsula, it was quickly confronted with a whole series of new problems as it spread into the more settled societies formerly controlled by the Sassanian Persian and Byzantine empires. The Arabs embarked upon conquest to gain booty and to spread their religion into new territories. Their unity, religious zeal, and desire for economic gain made them too powerful for the Persian and Byzantine empires. Both were rent with internal religious and political divisions. Their armies, so long used to exploiting subject peoples, were no match for the invaders. Many dependent peoples welcomed the invading Arab armies, hopeful for liberation from imperial oppression. The list of victories reveals the rapidity and ease with which the Arab armies completed their conquests: in 635 Damascus was taken, Egypt in 639, Persia in 640. North Africa was overrun during the next thirty years.

In most of its essentials the conquest of Egypt was typical of the

Arab-Muslim successes in the Middle East. The Arab army commanded by Amr ibn al-As was probably smaller than the Byzantine force garrisoned in Egypt. But already Egypt was torn by internal divisions, particularly by the discontent of the Coptic religious community under Byzantine rule. The political hierarchy established in Egypt had begun to fragment. The rulers, political and military alike, were largely independent both from Constantinople and from their superiors in Egypt. The imperial military forces were primarily interested in exploiting the local population and amassing personal wealth. The army in Egypt had long since ceased to act as a single unit and was incapable of defense against invasion. The one truly heroic effort by Cyrus to reorganize Egypt and to prepare both the political and military systems against a possible invasion was a failure because of internal opposition. The conquest, lasting over a two-year period, may have begun only as a raid for booty. But the Arab leaders knew the worth of Egypt, economically and politically, and saw the virtue of occupying and taking control of the country. According to one authority, the Arab general, Amr ibn al-As, had previously engaged in commercial undertakings in Egypt. There seems little doubt that Coptic hostility to Byzantine rule facilitated the Arab invasion. The Copts may have looked upon the Arab armies as mere plundering invaders and felt that this invading army would rid them of their Byzantine overlords.[1]

Although Egypt was conquered with ease, its subsequent reorganization and administration under Arab rule was a more difficult task. The conquerors were not experienced in the administration of settled and highly developed territories, let alone the vast territorial empire that they were overrunning. Indeed, they were not nearly so sophisticated in administrative, economic, and cultural matters as those they had conquered. They had few precedents to rely upon, for within the Arabian peninsula from which they came their basic social unit had been the tribe, whose organization was ill-suited to control the more highly developed economic and political institutions they had conquered.[2] During Muhammad's lifetime, in fact, the tribal organization had already begun to break down under economic pressure. The city of Mecca was becoming an important

[1] Emile Amelineau, "La Conquête de l'Egypte par les Arabes," *Revue Historique*, CXIX (1915), 273-310, and CXX (1915), 1-25.

[2] For a description of tribal organization in pre-Islamic Arabia see Emile Tyan, *Institutions du Droit Public Musulman: Le Califat* (Paris: 1954), pp. 3-116.

commercial center, and Medina was developing an agricultural economy. One of the chief emphases in Muhammad's new religion was the revitalization of the basic tribal ethics in a changing environment. Muhammad had provided a new basis of unity for his people, a unity founded more on religion than on tribe. He had also laid down in the Koran some fundamental social and personal principles by which men were to regulate their lives. These principles dealt mainly with religious duties—prayers, alms-giving, fasting—and with the regulation of personal life—marriage, divorce, wills, and testaments.[3] Islam was thus much more than just a religion; it was a total and universal way of life embracing man's political, social, and cultural requirements. Although it is clear that Muhammad gave to the Arabian community a sense of unity and a zeal to bring new territories under the Islamic banner, he did not give this community any kind of a comprehensive program for governing its newly conquered empire.

The overriding virtue of the Arab conquerors in the first half century was a clear recognition of their own limitations. The first four caliphs (632-61) and the early Umayyad rulers adopted many of the governing techniques of the preceding Byzantine and Persian empires. The Byzantine system of coinage was retained. The administrative language, Greek, was at first utilized. In the early stages of their rule the Arabs limited their interests to war, public order, religion, the distribution of pensions, and the collection of the tax on non-Muslims. Other branches of the administration, and in particular the collection of land taxes, were left in the hands of subject peoples.[4]

For its first thirty years the Islamic empire was controlled from the Arabian peninsula. With the triumph of the Umayyad dynasty (661-750) the seat of political authority was brought to Damascus and, thus, to one of the old centers of power and settled civilization. The Umayyads were also able to introduce a dynastic principle into the Caliphate. The founder of the dynasty was Muawiya, who capitalized on his strong position in Syria to overthrow the fourth caliph, Ali, and to install himself on the throne. The Umayyad victory of 661 was the "outcome of a coalition or compromise between those who

[3] W. Montgomery Watt, *Muhammad at Mecca* (Oxford: 1953) and *Muhammad at Medina* (Oxford: 1956).

[4] *Histoire Générale des Civilisations*, Vol. III, *Le Moyen Age*, Edouard Perroy, ed., p. 92. The sections on Islam in this volume are written by Claude Cahen.

represented the Islamic ideal of a religious community, united by common allegiance to the heritage of the Prophet, and the Meccan secular interpretation of unity, against the threat of anarchy implicit in tribalism." [5] The Umayyad dynasty controlled the Islamic empire until its overthrow by the Abbasids in 750. Umayyad rule was that of Arabs over non-Arab peoples. Although the Umayyad dynasty continued to make use of the subject peoples within the administration, the dominant ruling positions were held by the Arabs, and the empire was run for the benefit of the Arabs.

The Umayyads had triumphed, but they were not unopposed. Ali, the son-in-law of Muhammad, had claimed the Caliphate, and upon his death and the establishment of the Umayyad dynasty his followers, known as Shiites, continued to support the claims of the family of Ali to the Caliphate. In time the Shiites evolved into one of the important forces of political opposition within the Islamic world. Other groups—such as the Kharijites, who asserted that the Caliphate should not be conferred on the grounds of family and heredity but on the grounds of individual merit—were also political opponents of the orthodox community, but their followings were insignificant when compared with that of Shiism. The Shiites played an important role in the overthrow of the Umayyad dynasty, but they were, in turn, kept from power by the Abbasids, who became defenders of orthodox religion.

Egypt was but a province within a vast empire under the Umayyads and their Abbasid successors. During Umayyad rule, as one aphorism of the time recalled, it was Syria which governed, Iraq which opposed, and the Hijaz which collected the *hadith* (traditions from the Prophet).[6] Egypt had economic importance as a producer of cereals, a manufacturer of papyrus, and a payer of taxes, but as the aphorism indicates, it was not as influential as other parts of the empire at this time. In a revealing study of one of the governors of the province of Egypt, the French scholar Henri Lammens has described Egypt under Umayyad government:[7] Al-Qurra, governor of Egypt from 708 until 714, was a Syrian Arab, a qualification of great importance under the Umayyads. In Egypt his primary responsi-

[5] H. A. R. Gibb, "An Interpretation of Islamic History," in *Studies on the Civilization of Islam*, Stanford J. Shaw and William R. Polk, eds., p. 8.

[6] Henri Lammens, *Etudes sur le siècle des Omayyades* (Beirut: 1930), p. 313.

[7] *Ibid.*, 305-23; also H. I. Bell, "The Administration of Egypt under the Umayyad Khalifs," *Byzantinische Zeitschrift*, XXVIII (1928), 278-86.

bilities were the maintenance of order, the collection of taxes, and the proper functioning of the irrigation system on which the revenues of the state so largely depended. Taxes were high at this time, and many of the Egyptian *fellahin* (peasants) tried to evade them by deserting their fields. Thus, one of the additional responsibilities of the governor was to return fugitive peasants to their lands. In many respects Umayyad rule of the seventh century was not unlike British rule in Egypt many centuries later, for the Umayyads were occupying rulers, overlords, concerned primarily with certain key branches of the administration such as public works, order, and finances. Like the British, they garrisoned certain areas, spoke a different language from the mass of the population, and had a different religious system.

Toward the end of the seventh century there took place a pronounced Arabization and Islamization of the empire. These changes occurred in Egypt most noticeably during the reigns of Abd al-Malik ibn Marwan and his son al-Walid from 685 to 715. The first act was the suppression of Byzantine coinage and the introduction of Arab coins bearing the confession of the Muslim faith. In 706 Arabic was introduced as the administrative language. Recruitment into the upper branches of the administration was increasingly reserved for Muslims. There was now greater incentive to convert to Islam, and from this period the Coptic population first began to embrace the religion of their rulers.

The Umayyad empire was built on the twin foundations of Arab dominance and non-Arab submission. Cutting across these foundations, however, was the tenet of equality within Islam. Islam was a religion for all, and theoretically it was not to bring any kind of political or economic disability to non-Arab Muslims. The internal tension resulting from this contradiction was minimal as long as the vast majority of Muslims were Arabs. But as more and more of the subject peoples converted to Islam, demands for equal treatment became more intense. They resented the economic and political privileges reserved to the Arabs, and they began to agitate for alterations in the basic institutions of the Umayyad dynasty.

These problems were to prove the undoing of the Umayyad dynasty. The decline of this ruling elite was also accelerated by dissensions within it. The Arabs had never fully mastered the problem of running a complex administrative system. They had brought their own rudimentary political techniques with them into the more settled societies of the Middle East. They had relapsed into their tribal, factional, warring ways, and this disunity eventually enabled their opponents to mount a successful attack against them.[8] Opposition came from a coalition of religious leaders within the Arab-Islamic community and an Islamized landed aristocracy from Khurasan. In 750 the Umayyad dynasty was overthrown and supplanted by the Abbasids, a triumph for non-Arab factions. While racial lines continued to be important, the empire now became multiracial, based on the unity of religion and to a lesser extent on the unity of the Arabic language. The Abbasid dynasty also represented an important advance for the Persian tradition within Islam, especially in the administration and the organization of the Caliphate.

Throughout the Umayyad and the Abbasid periods there was a gradual elaboration of the institutions and ideals which came to be typical of medieval Islamic civilization. Over time the conquering Arabs merged their own experience with traditions borrowed from the Persian and Byzantine worlds. The Caliphate, for example, evolved as a combination of Arab with Persian and Byzantine models. At the death of Muhammad the leading members of the community met and selected Abu Bakr as Muhammad's successor. Three other caliphs were selected in much the same fashion, reminiscent of the selection of a tribal chief. The caliph was regarded at first as the successor of Muhammad; later as the representative, both religious and political, of God on earth. Under the Umayyads a dynastic principle based heavily on the Byzantine model was introduced. The Abbasid Caliphate strengthened the dynastic notion, adding to it, from Persian practices, the pomp, ceremony, despotism, and aura of the divine which had been characteristic of Persian rulers.

Another fast-changing institution was the system of Islamic law. The legal injunctions laid down by Muhammad were hardly comprehensive. Not surprisingly, these rudimentary guidelines were supplemented by other legal practices, many of which were absorbed from Byzantine and Persian legal procedures. The law was made primarily by the judges, who were only partially concerned to fit the legal system into the precepts and spirit of Islam. Schools of legal opinion gradually began to emerge, based in different geographical areas, and employing their own precedents and customs. The gradual

[8] This view is presented most clearly in Daniel C. Dennett, *Conversion and Poll Tax in Early Islam* (Cambridge: 1950). The more traditional emphasis on inequality in Islam as the basis for the downfall of the Umayyads can be found in J. Wellhausen, *The Arab Kingdom and Its Fall* (Calcutta: 1927).

Islamization of the empire brought a reaction against these rather permissive legal practices. New scholars tried to redefine the legal system more rigidly within the framework of Islam. Criticisms were launched against the idea of a living tradition, based upon the immediate precedents of communities. The new schools began to emphasize, as a fundamental source of the law, the sayings and stories attributed to the companions of the Prophet. Nevertheless, this development was but a temporary stage in the evolution of the Islamic legal system, known as the Sharia. New, more universal schools arose under the inspiration of great founders, the most astute of whom was al-Shafii. Al-Shafii held that there were only four basic sources for the law. These were, virtually in order of importance, the Koran, the traditions of the Prophet, the consensus of the orthodox community (generally expressed through its scholars), and the use of analogy. Al-Shafii's system was directed against the old legal schools with their emphasis on personal opinion and other nonreligious sources. Al-Shafii cast a dim eye on the sayings and traditions of the companions of the Prophet. For him the best source was the *hadith* (tradition) of the Prophet, handed down to the present generation through a faultless and unbroken chain of respected authorities. Al-Shafii's system postulated that the revelation of Muhammad was full and sufficient and should supplant personal opinion and the exercise of individual reason as a source for guidance in legal matters.[9] The work of al-Shafii led to energetic collections of *hadith* from the Prophet. Although many of these had been put into circulation by later generations, they were attributed to Muhammad, and a chain of authorities for the traditions was carefully worked out.

In such a fashion over a period of two and a half centuries the legal system in the Islamic empire was gradually brought under the control of Islamic scholars and linked with the religious disciplines. Its sources were defined in an orthodox fashion, allowing little room for the exercise of free interpretation or, of course, for the operation of the concept that man's condition might be a changing one requiring new legal standards. By the same token, the theological character of Islamic law (that is, purely religious law) contributed to the emergence of administrative, military, and political law. Whereas religious law was an instrument of the scholarly, religious class,

[9] See Joseph Schacht, *The Origins of Mohammedan Jurisprudence* (Oxford: 1950) and *Esquisse d'une histoire du droit musulman* (Paris: 1953).

political and military elites within the empire developed their own law. Between these two important groups and these two prevailing systems of law there was often considerable tension, and, not surprisingly, separate and sometimes contradictory development. Nevertheless, the men of religion always asserted that the Sharia was all-inclusive. The most significant development of administrative and military law took place under the Ottoman empire, which from its origins in the fourteenth century was required to exert control over far-flung territories. Although the Ottomans regarded themselves as orthodox Muslims and upholders of the Islamic legal system, they helped to develop flexibility within their administrative system through the issuance of sultanic, nonreligious law.

There was a similar evolution of thought in the theological and philosophical realm, a similar emphasis on the Islamization of foreign elements, and thus on internal consistency. The early Muslims were deeply influenced by Greek thought. Most translations from Greek were made by Arabic-speaking Christians in the service of Muslim political and cultural leaders, and Greek science and philosophy, particularly the works of Aristotle, were thereby made available to the Arabs. For some Muslims Greek thought led to free thought, perhaps even agnosticism. Most of the philosophers in the orthodox community, however, employed Greek philosophical models and methods in defense of the faith. The major philosophical controversies revolved around the nature and power of God and man's own responsibility and free will. An influential sect of speculative theology was that of the Mutazilites. Using Greek philosophy to combat the heretical and anti-Arab tendencies among Persian philosophers, these thinkers emphasized man's free will and his responsibility for actions. The Mutazila school was, for a time, closely tied to the Abbasid Caliphate and was a powerful force in combatting heresy. Within the Mutazila school there was a reaction against some of its more liberal ideas, a reaction which culminated in the theological writings of al-Ashari (873-941). While accepting many of the basic ideas and methods of the Mutazilites, al-Ashari placed his primary emphasis on God's omnipotence and man's weakness. For al-Ashari man's actions were preordained by an all-powerful God, and man's knowledge of God was quite limited. The Asharite system of thought, with its emphasis on the frailty of human endeavor and reason, became an important theological system for much of medieval Islam.

As early as the Abbasid seizure of power in 750 the Islamic empire, which stretched from the Atlantic Coast to Central Asia, had begun to fragment. One of the Umayyad heirs to the throne had managed to escape the avenging hand of the Abbasids. Fleeing across North Africa, he succeeded in establishing an independent dynasty in Spain. Still, in the eighth century and the first part of the ninth century the fragmentation was confined to the peripheries of the Islamic world—Spain, North Africa, and parts of Eastern Asia. It was not until the latter half of the ninth century that these tensions became apparent in the heart of Islam, and particularly in Egypt.

The French scholar Claude Cahen has sought to compare medieval Islamic civilization with medieval Europe.[10] Although observing some striking differences, particularly in landholding practices, feudal obligations, and the presence of nomads, the author emphasizes the great similarities between the societies. Both had roughly the same technological base, the same primary emphasis on agriculture, the same development of a middle or commercial class. According to Cahen, the decisive event which altered the direction of Islamic history and distinguished it from medieval Europe was the emergence in the ninth and tenth centuries of powerful military autocracies. Internal power struggles led to the creation of these groups. To increase political security in the face of opposition, the ruling civilian elements supplanted the old conscripted Arab armies with professional military groups, largely recruited from the Turkish tribes of Central Asia. In time these professional military cadres became so powerful that the civil administration could no longer dominate them. Although one military dynasty competed with another and there were frequent changes of rulers, the dominance of military oligarchies continued. The financial demands of these military elites precipitated revolts, which only strengthened the military class and not infrequently resulted in even greater impositions upon civilian populations. Military autocracies soon emerged to dominate the other groups and classes in the Islamic world. They ruthlessly exploited their provinces, subordinating the peasantry and commercial classes and thus precluding the development of an independent middle class. During this period land concessions, known as *iqta*, were made to high military officers, many of whom were able

[10] Claude Cahen, "L'Evolution Sociale du Monde Musulman jusqu'au XII° Siècle face à celle du Monde Chrétien, *Cahiers de Civilisation Médiévale*, I (1958), 451-63, and II (1959), 37-51.

to acquire considerable political authority over the inhabitants as well. The military officers especially suppressed the peasantry, the source of their own wealth, and deprived them of the little freedom that they had previously enjoyed.

In Egypt rule by a professionalized and alien military caste began with the short-lived but influential Tulunid dynasty (868-905). The founder of the dynasty, Ahmad ibn Tulun, was a Turk reared in the Abbasid court at Samarra. His father had been taken as a slave from Central Asia and sent by the prefect of Bukhara to the caliph. The Abbasid rulers were fast becoming dependent upon their Persian ministers and their Turkish army officers, and as a favorite and a talented young man, Ahmad ibn Tulun was dispatched to govern the province of Egypt. There, after a short, bitter struggle with his rivals, he was able to consolidate his power. He reorganized the army and administrative system, and then proclaimed Egypt's independence from Abbasid control. Displaying that fatal fascination for Syria which has gripped Egypt's rulers since Pharaonic times, he attacked Syria and established Egyptian rule. Beset by serious internal divisions, the Abbasids were in no position to resist, and Ahmad ibn Tulun's successor, Khumarawaih, subsequently exacted recognition of Egyptian autonomy from the Abbasid caliph.

Although a military regime, the ruling Tulunid military caste was not entirely composed of alien Turkish and Circassian soldiers brought into Egypt from the outside. To be sure, important positions in the army and the administration were reserved for the Turks; the Arabs, on the other hand, no longer retained their dominant position, for they had intermingled with the indigenous population and become part of it. Actually, the army was composed mostly of mercenaries—Greeks, Negroes, Turks, and some Arabs. Turkish influence was only a thin veneer on the top of Egyptian society, symbolized by the court life, in which Ahmad ibn Tulun and his successors emulated that of the Abbasids at Samarra.

The Tulunid dynasty lasted only until 905. By that time the Abbasids had regrouped their forces and were able to launch a successful invasion of Egypt. Moreover, the Tulunids were beset by a number of problems, not unlike those of other military dynasties within the Muslim world. Ahmad ibn Tulun's successors were not men of his own caliber. They allowed administrative and military matters to slip from their grasp. The army grew discontented, and factions appeared within it and within the administration. As the pace of conquest slowed and the amount of booty decreased, the military became particularly rebellious. The Egyptian rulers found themselves hard pressed to cope with Shiite uprisings in Syria.[11]

Although short-lived, the Tulunid dynasty was a harbinger of the future development of military regimes. It also revealed the growing weakness and fragmentation of the Islamic empire. The peripheral regions had already been lost to independent regimes. With the advent of an independent state in Egypt the very center of the empire itself was now in the process of dissolution. Despite the defeat of the Tulunids, the Abbasids were unable to check the disintegration, and a new independent but alien dynasty, the Ikhshidids, reestablished the autonomy of Egypt for a short period. They were followed by an even more aggressive ruling elite, the Fatimids, who not only held Egypt independent from the Eastern centers of power but even threatened to reorganize Islam from Egypt under a new set of institutions based on the heretical Shiism, in contrast to those of the orthodox Abbasid caliphs.

Although later influenced by the popular doctrines of Islamic mysticism, called Sufiism, it still remains something of a paradox that Shiism, with its narrow political doctrine—the notion that the Caliphate should belong exclusively to the family of Ali—should have attracted such a widespread following. But this it did. It had great appeal among different groups in Persia and North Africa, and among the lower social orders in the cities and villages. Political opposition, often drawing support from economic grievances, usually used the banner of Shiism against the Sunnites, those who acknowledged the first four caliphs as the legitimate successors of Muhammad. Shiite Islam was distinguished theologically and politically from Sunni Islam by its emphasis on the role of the *imam* and by its esoteric doctrines. The Shiites had been influenced by Greek thought, particularly the transcendentalist and emanationist ideas of Neoplatonic thought. Like the Neoplatonists, they believed that the universe had issued from a universal reason and was controlled by the principle of universal reason. All of the universe was composed of universal reason, but to varying degrees, matter having only small quantities of it. The religious organization was hierarchical and elitist; individuals rose through training and action to the higher

[11] Zaky Mohamed Hassan, Les Tulunids: Etude de l'Egypte Musulmane à la Fin du IX° Siècle, 868-905 (Paris: 1933).

orders as they were thought to come closer to an understanding of the principle of universal reason. At the pinnacle of this religious hierarchy was the *imam*, either the direct descendant of Ali or his representative on earth. Through his birth or through his commission, the *imam* was regarded as being capable of interpreting universal reason to the rest of the community and of being able to understand and make known the esoteric truths of the universe. Certain Shiite groups were further characterized by extreme activism; one of their important religious orders was that of the missionary (*dai*), who was expected to go out and to convert others to his creed. Some Shiite groups, however, were quietist.

Like Sunnism, Shiism was a fragmented religious and political movement divided into numerous sects, each of which derived its authority from a different line of succession from Ali. In this early period the groups known as the Sevener Shiites or Ismailis were the most influential. Their adherents had broken from the others over the question of the succession to the seventh *imam*, hence their name, the Seveners. There were four distinct groups within this movement: the early Ismailis, the Fatimid Ismailis, the Syro-Mesopotamian Carmatians, and the Carmatians of Bahrayn.[12] The Carmatians were the most radical, for they espoused social egalitarian ideals. They were open and aggressive in their attacks on the Sunni community, organizing themselves into armed bands and establishing centers of power in Iraq, Syria, and Bahrayn. Moreover, their appeal was specifically directed to the suppressed and displaced lower classes within the Islamic empire.

A more sophisticated and subtle form of Ismailism was the Fatimid movement. It spread into North Africa, where the Fatimids created a dynasty to rival Abbasid power in Asia. Under the leadership of their general, Jawhar, the Fatimids conquered Egypt in 969 and established their center of power there. From Egypt the dynasty sent out missionaries into Asia to convert Muslims to its doctrines. Shiism, and the Fatimids in particular, had a strong appeal in Persia, Iraq, and Syria, where Shiite ideas had already taken hold. The Fatimids ruled Egypt and parts of North Africa and Syria from 969 until 1171. As many scholars have pointed out, Shiism as practiced by the Fatimids in Egypt did not penetrate to the population, having meaning to only a thin veneer of scholars, religious leaders, and

[12] Bernard Lewis, *The Origins of Ismailism* (Cambridge: 1940).

administrators.[13] But in the struggle for political power with the Abbasids in Asia, Fatimid Egypt came into its own as a center of political authority, commerce, and scholarship. Jawhar founded the city of Cairo, an extension of Fustat, the old capital, and al-Azhar was established as a center of Islamic learning. The Fatimid regime was also characterized by great toleration for Christians and by its vigorous intellectual life.

In the eleventh and twelfth centuries the Fatimid dynasty began to decline. The spirit of the regime depended on its ideology and on its ability to spread its doctrines into new areas. The Fatimids were frustrated in their efforts to overthrow Sunnism throughout Asia, and the Ismaili-Fatimid movement became increasingly torn by factionalism. Many of the Egyptian administrators had grown complacent because of the successes already attained, but they were challenged by ideologues and extremists. The later years of the dynasty were marked by ideological disputes within Egypt inspired by Persian Shiites who had migrated to Egypt. In 1016 there was an influx of Persian extremists into Egypt whose intention was to convince Caliph al-Hakim (996-1021) of his divinity.[14] Egypt was fairly unreceptive to these ideas, and the extremist leaders began to proselytize elsewhere. In the reign of al-Mustansir (1036-94) Fatimid power began to disintegrate, and the Fatimid movement fragmented into extreme revolutionary sects like the Nusayris in Syria and the Assassins in Persia.

Another important factor in the decline of the Fatimids and Shiism in general was the rise of the Seljuk Turks, who entered the Islamic empire from Central Asia in the tenth century. Their three great military leaders, Tughril (1037-63), Alp Arslan (1063-72), and Malikshah (1072-92), brought much of the heartland of Islam under their control. The Seljuks were militant exponents of orthodoxy. They opened schools (madrasahs) to turn out scholars and combatted Shiism on both the political and intellectual planes.

During this theologically turbulent period Shiism was also influenced by the growing power of Sufism, Islamic mysticism, which emphasized emotional and personal experiences of God. Mainly the work of individual religious figures in early centuries, Sufi mysticism

<hr>

[13] Claude Cahen, "Doctrines Religieuses," *L'Elaboration de l'Islam* (Paris: 1961), p. 13.

[14] P. J. Vatikiotis, "The Rise of Extremist Sects and the Dissolution of the Fatimid Empire in Egypt," *Islamic Culture*, XXXI, No. 1 (1957), 17-26.

began to penetrate urban and rural masses, where it achieved a wide-spread following. The participants were organized into orders or brotherhoods, each with its own distinctive rituals and ceremonies. Although Sufism probably had a greater appeal to Turkish and Berber groups, it was widespread among the Arab population as well. The Sufi orders generally were not opposed to orthodoxy, for the established powers—the scholars and the military and administrative leaders—instead of rejecting it as heresy, saw fit to approve it.[15] Nevertheless, Sufi mysticism appears to have been more hindrance than help to the extension of Shiite power, which in Egypt could not withstand the military strength of the Ayyubid dynasty. Although there were still important centers of Shiism, even the founding of a powerful and independent Shiite dynasty in Persia under the Safa-wids, its bid for dominance had been defeated.

Within Egypt the successors to the Fatimids were Kurdish military leaders who formed the Ayyubid dynasty (1171-1254). Although the Ayyubids were not always on the best terms with Seljuks, they did model their administration after Seljuk practice. Their administrators seem to have been influenced by the famous political treatise writ-ten by Nizam al-Mulk, which served as a political guide for the Seljuks. They also introduced the *madrasah* system into Egypt and made al-Azhar into a center of orthodox learning, indeed one of the great educational centers in the Islamic world. The Ayyubid dy-nasty arose from the Syrian empire of Nur al-Din; Egypt, a rebellious province, was held loosely. Nur al-Din's lieutenant in Egypt was the famous Saladin, who was able to assert his independence from Syria upon Nur al-Din's death. Saladin's major contribution to Islamic political history was, of course, his successful wars and treaties against the European crusaders, for he drove the crusaders from the interior of Egypt and Syria, confining their territorial administration to the coastal regions of these countries. Saladin also carried on the defense of orthodox Islam against Shiism, and he forced the Shiite bands into small mountain fortresses and enclaves where they constituted a lesser threat to the Sunni political order than in the past.[16]

[15] H. A. R. Gibb regards Sufism as a true revolution in Islam, for he writes that "through the influence of Sufism the Islamic world was entirely transformed from the thirteenth century onward—spiritually, morally, intellectually, imagina-tively, and even politically—and only the orthodox madrasas preserved a tenuous link with the cultural tradition of medieval Islam." *Studies on Civilization of Islam*, p. 32.

[16] Gibb, "The Achievement of Saladin," in *Studies on the Civilization of Islam*.

Ayyubid rule was followed by one of the most remarkable military oligarchies in Egyptian history, that of the Mamluks (1254-1517). In Arabic *Mamluk* means slave, and the Mamluk empire was run by Turkish, Circassian, Greek, and Kurdish slaves imported by the ruling groups in Egypt mainly from the Caspian and the Caucasus. These slaves were taken as boys from their families, and, having been brought to Egypt, they were attached to a ruling Mamluk group and given a military training. Upon the completion of their training they joined one of the many Mamluk armies and gradually struggled up the hierarchy of power. The Mamluk period has been divided into two parts, the latter one called the Circassian era because the most powerful Mamluks were drawn almost exclusively from that group.

Under Mamluk and later during Ottoman rule Egypt felt the full force of alien, military domination. Native-born Egyptians were restricted to minor administrative posts designed to keep the administrative machinery functioning for the benefit of their Mamluk overlords.[17] The Mamluks themselves virtually monopolized the armed forces and the art of war. They were divided into various military units, often at odds with one another. The most powerful, influential, and wealthy were the royal Mamluks, Mamluks who passed into the service of the reigning sultan from other masters or who were the actual Mamluks of the ruler. They formed the backbone of the Mamluk army and numbered about ten thousand. They bore the brunt of the fighting, owned the largest feudal estates, and from among them were appointed the *amirs*, the military commanders. The other powerful groups were the Mamluks of the *amirs* themselves. There was considerable competition for power among these units, especially when a ruler died and was replaced by a new sultan. When this occurred, the new ruler attempted to solidify

[17] The major exception to this statement was the *halqa*, a corps of free, non-Mamluk cavalry. The *halqa* was most honored in the time of Saladin. In the early years of the Mamluk era it preserved its power and lofty position, but declined as the royal Mamluks rose in prestige. Within the *halqa* were the sons of Mamluks, born as free men and as Muslims. As the organization began to decline, it was infiltrated by merchants and artisans who had paid their way into the ranks in order to improve their social status. David Ayalon, "The System of Payment in Mamluk Military Society," *Journal of Economic and Social History of the Orient*, I (1957), 37-65, 257-96; "Studies on the Structure of the Mamluk Army," *Bulletin of the School of Oriental and African Studies*, XV (1953), 203-28, 448-76, and XVI (1954), 57-90.

power by promoting his own followers into important positions and by removing Mamluks of the previous ruler from them.

Mamluk rule was designed to siphon off as much wealth for the ruling elite as possible. The country was divided into provinces. These were put under the control of Mamluk *amirs*, and the revenue from them was divided among the Mamluk troops. The lion's share went, of course, to the sultan and his Mamluks. It was the duty of the administration to maintain public security, to keep the irrigation system in good working order, and to collect taxes. This complex administrative system was controlled from Cairo. In fact, the central government's control of lands allocated to provincial administrators was a feature that distinguished the Mamluk political system from other more fragmented and less centralized political structures throughout the Islamic world. The Mamluk overlords obtained sizeable amounts of wealth from the land and also from the considerable mercantile activity of Egypt.

The true founder of the Mamluk dynasty was the famed Baybars (1260-77). Not only did he crystallize the system of importing young boys from Asia—a system which had already been gaining popularity throughout the Islamic world—but, more important for the future security of the Mamluk regime, he defended Egypt from its external enemies. To Baybars belongs the credit of completing the task begun by Saladin. He drove back the crusaders from Egypt. Considerably more formidable was the threat of the Mongols. Indeed, the Mamluks for a long time lived under the shadow of this conquering force which had swept across Muslim Asia, bringing destruction to its centers of civilization and administration. The Mamluk dynasty served as a barrier against the further westward advance of the Mongols, and their defeat of the Mongols secured Egypt and elevated the country to the first rank among Muslim states independent of Mongol control.

The decline of the Mamluk regime was hastened by the advent of the Circassian period. Despite Turkish resistance the Circassian element assumed supremacy in Egypt at the end of the fourteenth century. This group maintained close ties with their families in the Caucasus and brought over their young men. Ethnic origins became the primary consideration for military preferment. During the Circassian period no Turk became sultan. The Circassians also curtailed the period of study in the military school and admitted a large proportion of adults to the Mamluk corps. Within the Mamluk corps promotion depended less on demonstrated ability and obedience than on family ties. Another factor in the decline of the Mamluks was their inability to adapt to advancing military technology as readily as their opponents. Although they had some knowledge of firearms, their entire military strategy revolved around the use of cavalry troops, the supreme military unit of the Mamluk warriors. Consequently, they did not assimilate the use of firearms into their military program. In their military encounters with the rising power of the Middle East, the Ottomans, they were unable to withstand the superior firepower of Ottoman infantrymen. In 1516 north of Aleppo the famed Mamluk cavalry was easily destroyed by Ottoman troops at the battle of Marj Dabiq.[18]

Egypt's commercial role was always important in the medieval period. From Fatimid times until the decline of the Mamluks the country was an especially vigorous entrepot of trade between East and West. From the East—India, China, and Indonesia—Muslim traders brought peppers, spices, textiles, silk, and many other products. These goods were traded throughout the Muslim world or were exported to European merchants from Mediterranean countries. The Muslim countries also exported to Europe manufactured products, especially textiles. Egypt was central in all of these trading patterns, for the peoples of the Middle East—Jews, Christians, and Muslims alike—virtually monopolized the long and difficult trade routes to the East. Traveling with the monsoon winds, sailing ships brought their goods from the East first to Aden or Yemen and then across to the Egyptian-Sudanese coast. From there the traders went inland to the Nile and down the Nile to Cairo. In the Mamluk period the so-called Karimi merchants were the dominant commercial figures in this trade and actually monopolized the trade in spices. Scholars have found no satisfactory meaning for the word *Karim*. They have found evidence of Karimi merchants as early as the Fatimid period, and there seems reason to believe that the word at that time meant convoy. The activities of the Karimi merchants reached their height during the Mamluk period, during which time they were organized into a great corporation or guild for controlling the Eastern trade. Many of the merchants came originally from Yemen, but their base of operations was Egypt. For a long time the Mamluk regime gave

[18] David Ayalon, *Gunpowder and Firearms in the Mamluk Kingdom* (London: 1956).

the Karimi merchants considerable freedom, allowing them to dominate the trade with the East.[19] Toward the end of the period the Mamluk rulers moved to take over these mercantile operations, motivated by the desire to increase state revenues for their heavy military expenditures. The truly decisive blow to Egyptian commerce was the emergence of the Portuguese in the Indian Ocean at the end of the fifteenth century. Within a short time the Portuguese had supplanted the Arabs as merchants and traders between East and West.

Sporadic rebellions of the governed population challenged the military regimes in Egypt. These rebellions were in no sense revolutions.[20] The rebels had no intention of overthrowing the regime, of establishing a new form of government, of introducing new political institutions, or of altering in any fundamental manner the essential relationship between the governed and the governing. The rebellions were designed to produce minor political and economic adjustments. Generally, they involved three groups—peasants, beduins, and an urban proletariat of slaves, free workmen, and artisans. The city revolts were usually outbursts of the poor seeking a reduction in the food prices or the discharge of a hated official. The rebellions commonly occurred during times of economic distress. In the countryside the rebels withheld essential food products from the cities and ruling elites. Frequently the rural revolts were led by beduins and resulted in the granting of political and economic concessions to the beduin groups. The one group that invariably did not derive any benefit from rebellion was the peasantry, who were kept at their minimum standards of life.

The Ottoman conquest of Egypt in 1517 was not as decisive an event as might appear, for in reality the influence of the Mamluks was not totally eradicated, and Egypt was at first permitted to enjoy considerable autonomy within the Ottoman empire. Indeed, the original goal of the Ottomans was to overthrow the ruling Mamluk faction, deemed inimical to Ottoman aims, and to supplant it with

[19] S. D. Goitein, "New Light on the Beginnings of the Karim Merchants," *Journal of the Economic and Social History of the Orient*, I (1958), 175-84. Slightly differing interpretations are found in Walter J. Fischel, "The Spice Trade in Mamluk Egypt," *Journal of the Economic and Social History of the Orient*, I (1958), 157-74, and E. Ashtor, "The Karimi Merchants," *Journal of the Royal Asiatic Society* (1956), 45-56.

[20] A. N. Poliak, "Les Révoltes Populaires en Egypte à l'Epoque des Mamelouks et leurs causes économiques," *Revue des Etudes Islamiques*, VIII (1934), 251-73.

a more friendly faction. Following the defeat of the Mamluk ruler the Ottoman Sultan Selim appointed Khair Bey, a Mamluk, as his viceroy in Egypt. This system of utilizing Mamluks to govern Egypt proved short-lived, however. Upon the death of Khair Bey, Egypt was torn by revolts as Mamluk leaders vied for power and threatened to cast off Ottoman suzerainty. Selim's successor, Sulayman the Magnificent, finally decided to bring the province more firmly under Ottoman rule. He dispatched to Egypt his grand vizier, Ibrahim Pasha, who issued decrees to control the internal administration of Egypt. Egypt was now to be governed by a viceroy, appointed by the sultan in Istanbul. The Ottoman army was to be garrisoned in Egypt, and, in addition to supporting this army, Egypt was to pay tribute to Istanbul as a province of the Ottoman empire.

For the greater part of the sixteenth century the administrative system of Ibrahim Pasha effectively ruled Egypt. The country was administered as a province of the empire, under the domination of the sultan's agent serving as governor in Cairo. Toward the end of the century other ruling elements began to assert themselves. Among these were the Ottoman troops garrisoned in Egypt and various Mamluk factions. The practice of importing slaves into Egypt and attaching them to certain ruling groups had continued during the Ottoman period. Throughout the seventeenth and eighteenth centuries Egypt experienced numerous political conflicts as factions competed for control of the administrative structure, and soon the Ottoman delegate from Istanbul became a mere figurehead incapable of opposing the important military cliques. Political instability led to rural insecurity and economic decline. Egypt in the eighteenth century was clearly not as prosperous as it had been in the earlier Muslim periods.

At the end of the eighteenth century certain salient characteristics conditioned life in Egypt. Islamic law, although not totally pervasive or comprehensive, ruled the personal lives of the people. The minority Coptic community was granted tolerance, as was the custom within Islam, and its members were permitted to hold minor administrative posts. Nevertheless, the Copts paid a special tax reserved for non-Muslim communities. The exploitive military regimes of Egypt were also characteristic of other Muslim areas but were distinctive because of their greater administrative centralization, doubtless a result of the unity of the Nile Valley and the requirements of Egypt's complex irrigation system. The military authorities with power to collect taxes were not independent rulers of these tax territories but were under the control of the central government. Upper Egypt, however, was often in rebellion from the central government. The beduin tribes there were difficult to control, and defeated factions within the ruling elite often took refuge in Upper Egypt to regroup their forces.

Among the least developed of Egyptian institutions were those of the agricultural sector in which the vast majority of the population lived. Almost all that the peasants produced above their basic needs was taken by the ruling elites. The agricultural economy was not a specialized one. Cash crops were not grown, products were generally bartered between areas, and there was no highly developed or refined system of exchange. The major exception to this picture of a non-specialized and underdeveloped agricultural economy was the irrigation system. Since the economic wealth of Egypt depended upon the control of the Nile and its floodwaters, the irrigation system was of special interest to the central government. It was run with great skill and care, except in times of general political and economic instability. In contrast to agriculture, administrative and military institutions of the ruling elite were highly developed. Recruitment into these institutions at the higher levels was practically closed to the mass of the population, although certain groups, particularly the Copts, were permitted to staff the lower administrative rungs. Training for the administration and military was given in the schools and colleges of Egypt. Thus, although recruitment into the administration and army was reserved for certain groups, merit and ability were the criteria of advancement. Yet another important and highly developed group in Egypt was the middle class. Until the breakthrough of the Portuguese into the Indian Ocean, Egypt was one of the centers of a developed and specialized trading economy between East and West. The Egyptian commercial class was, consequently, an influential group, but one which could not aspire to the ruling elite. Its wealth was always subject to confiscation at the hands of the more powerful ruling groups. Finally, the numerous religious institutions had evolved into well developed organizations whose members served as judges, *imams*, teachers, and scholars in the *madrasahs* and other religious schools. In general, the members of the religious institutions came from the upper classes, but as religious schools were located in many villages, it was one institution through which members of the lower class could rise to positions of authority and influence.

The Sudan to 1821

The earliest inhabitants of the Sudan can be traced to ancient Negroid peoples who lived in the vicinity of Khartoum in mesolithic (middle stone age) times. They were hunters and gatherers who made combed pottery and later sandstone grinders. Toward the end of the neolithic (later stone age) they had domesticated animals. Moreover, these Negroid peoples were clearly in contact with predynastic civilizations to the north in Egypt, but the arid uplands between the first cataract of the Nile at Aswan and the gateway to the Sudan at Wadi Halfa appear to have discouraged the predynastic Egyptians from settling in Nubia. At the end of the fourth millennium B.C. kings of the First Dynasty conquered upper Nubia beyond Aswan, introducing Egyptian cultural influence to a non-Negroid people who were scattered along the river bank. In subsequent centuries Nubia was subjected to successive military expeditions from Egypt in search of slaves or building materials for Pharaonic tombs, destroying much of the Egyptian-Nubian culture that had sprung from the initial conquests of the First Dynasty. Throughout these five centuries (2800-2300 B.C.) the descendants of the Nubians continued to eke out an existence on the Nile, an easy prey to Egyptian military expeditions.

Sometime after 2300 B.C., in the period known to Egyptologists as the First Intermediate Dynasty (between the Sixth Dynasty and the rise of the Eleventh), a new wave of immigrants entered Nubia from the west, from Libya, where the increasing desiccation of the Sahara drove them to settle along the Nile as cattle farmers. Other branches of these people seem to have gone beyond the Nile to the Red Sea Hills, while still others pushed south and west to Wadai and Darfur. These newcomers were able to settle on the Nile and assimilate the existing Nubians without opposition from Egypt. After the fall of the Sixth Dynasty in 2300 B.C. Egypt experienced a century and a half of weakness and internal strife, permitting the immigrants in Nubia the time to develop their own distinct civilization with unique crafts, architecture, and social structure virtually unhindered by the potentially more dynamic civilization to the north. With the advent of the Eleventh Dynasty, however, Egypt recovered her strength and pressed southward into Nubia, at first sending only sporadic expeditions to exact tribute, but by the Twelfth Dynasty effectively occupying Nubia as far south as Semna. The Nubians resisted the Egyptian occupation, which was only maintained by a chain of forts erected along the Nile. Egyptian military and trading expeditions, of course, penetrated beyond Semna, and Egyptian fortified trading posts were actually established to the south at Kerma against frequent attacks upon Egyptian trading vessels by Nubian tribesmen beyond the southern frontier.

Despite the Egyptian presence in upper Nubia, the indigenous culture of the region continued to flourish little changed by the proximity of Egyptian garrisons or the imports of luxury articles by Egyptian traders. Indeed, the Egyptianization of Nubia appears to have been enhanced during the decline in Egypt's political control over Nubia during the Second Intermediate Period (c. 1780-1580 B.C.), when Nubians were employed in large numbers as mercenaries against the Asiatic Hyksos. Their return to Nubia did more to introduce Egyptian culture, which they had absorbed while fighting in Egyptian armies, than the centuries of Egyptian military occupation which they had resisted. The defeat of the Hyksos was the result of a national rising of the Egyptians who, once they had expelled the Hyksos from the Nile Valley, turned their energies southward to reestablish the military occupation of Nubia which the Hyksos invasion had disrupted. Under Tuthmosis I (1530-1520 B.C.) the Egyptian conquest of the Northern Sudan was completed as far as Kurgus, fifty miles south of Abu Hamad, and subsequent Egyptian military expeditions penetrated even farther up the Nile to the "land of the blacks." This third Egyptian occupation was the most complete and the most enduring, for despite sporadic rebellions against Egyptian control Nubia was deeply influenced by Egyptian culture. Nubia was divided into two administrative units, Wawat in the north with its provincial capital at Aswan, and Kush in the south with its headquarters at Napata (Marawi). A viceroy, usually a member of the royal entourage, was responsible to the Pharaoh. Under him were two deputies, one for Wawat and one for Kush, and a hierarchy of lesser officials. The bureaucracy was staffed chiefly by Egyptians, but Egyptianized Nubians were not uncommon. Colonies of Egyptian officials, traders, and priests surrounded the administrative centers, but beyond these outposts of Egyptian culture the Nubians continued to preserve their own distinct traditions, customs, and crafts. To the Egyptians, Nubia remained a foreign land.

But if Nubia was a foreign land, it was a rich one. Its position athwart the trade routes from Egypt to the Red Sea and Punt and from the Nile to the south and west brought great wealth from far-off places. Moreover, its cultivations along the Nile were rich, while in the hills the gold and emerald mines produced bullion and jewels for Egypt. The Nubians were renowned as soldiers. Thus, as Egypt slipped once again into decline at the close of the New Kingdom, the viceroys of Kush, supported by their Nubian levies, became virtually independent kings no longer appointed from Egypt. By the eighth century B.C. the kings of Kush came from hereditary ruling families of Egyptianized Nubian chiefs who possessed neither political nor family ties with Egypt. Under one such king, Kashta, Kush acquired control of Upper Egypt, and under his son Piankhy (751-716 B.C.) the whole of Egypt to the shores of the Mediterranean was brought under the administration of Kush. As a world power, however, Kush was not to last. Just when the kings of Kush had established their rule from Abu Hamad to the delta, the Assyrians invaded Egypt (671 B.C.) and with their superior iron-forged weapons defeated the armies of Kush under the redoubtable Taharqa; by 654 B.C. the kings had been driven back to Nubia and the safety of their capital, Napata. The glorious days of Kush as a Mediterranean state had come to an end.

Although reduced from a great power to an isolated kingdom behind the barren hills which blocked the southward advance from Aswan, Kush continued to rule over the middle Nile for another thousand years, its unique Egyptian-Nubian culture preserved while that of Egypt came under strange and alien influences. Although Egyptianized in many ways, the culture of Kush was not simply Egyptian civilization in a Nubian environment. The Kushites developed their own language, expressed first by Egyptian hieroglyphs, then their own, and finally by a cursive script. They worshiped Egyptian gods but did not abandon their own. They buried their kings in pyramids but not in the Egyptian fashion. Their wealth continued to flow from the mines and to grow with their control of the trade routes. Soon after the retreat from Egypt the capital was moved from Napata southward to Meroe near Shandi, where Kush was increasingly exposed to the Negroid, African cultures farther south at the very time when her ties with Egypt were rapidly disappearing. The subsequent history of Kush is one of gradual decay, quickened in the Christian era, and ending with inglorious extinction in 350 A.D. by the king of Axum who marched down from the Ethiopian highlands, destroyed Meroe, and sacked the decrepit riverine towns.

Although Kush was destroyed, its influence did not die. The remnants of Kushitic culture were scattered up the Nile and westward to the Niger and beyond. Kush had preserved its Egyptian-Nubian culture at the time when Pharaonic Egypt's was suffused by Greek and Roman influences, and she transmitted this culture, particularly the technique of ironworking, into Africa. Having learned to smelt iron from the Assyrian invaders, the Kushites developed at Meroe in the centuries before Christ an iron technology of which the huge slag piles of the "Birmingham of Africa" are today a stark reminder. From the time of Kush, Africa moved directly from the stone age to the iron age. Moreover, Kushitic political ideas and institutions also appear to have filtered west and south to influence the evolution of African culture. These were great contributions to the development of Africa, and "with Meroe, one may reasonably say, the history of modern Africa has begun." [21]

The two hundred years from the fall of Kush to the middle of the sixth century is an unknown age in the Sudan. Nubia was inhabited by a people called the Nobatae by the ancient geographers and the X-Group by modern archaeologists, who are still at a loss to explain their origins. The X-Group were clearly, however, the heirs of Kush, for their whole cultural life was dominated by Meroitic crafts and customs, and occasionally they even felt themselves sufficiently strong, in alliance with the nomadic Blemmyes (the ancient name for Beja) of the eastern Sudan, to attack the Romans in Upper Egypt. As was their habit, the Romans retaliated, defeating the Nobatae and Blemmyes and driving them into obscurity once again. When the Sudan was once more brought into the orbit of the Mediterranean world by the arrival of Christian missionaries in the sixth century, the middle Nile was divided into three kingdoms: Nobatia with its capital at Bukharas (modern Faras), Maqurra with its capital at old Dunqula, and the kingdom of Alwa in the south with its capital at Suba near Khartoum. Between 543 and 575 these three kingdoms were converted to Christianity by the work of Julian, who proselytized among the Nobatia (543-45), and his successor Longinus, who between 569 and 575 consolidated the work of Julian in Nobatia and even carried Christianity to Alwa in the south. The new religion appears to have been adopted with enthusiasm. Christian churches sprang up along the Nile, and ancient temples were refurbished to accommodate Christian worshipers. After the

[21] Basil Davidson, *Old Africa Rediscovered* (London: 1961), p. 60.

retirement of Longinus, however, the Sudan once again receded into a period about which we know little and did not reemerge into the stream of recorded history until the coming of the Arabs in the middle of the seventh century.

After the death of the Prophet Muhammad in 632 A.D., the Arabs erupted from the desert steppes of Arabia and overran the lands to the east and to the west. Egypt was invaded in 639, and small groups of Arab raiders penetrated up the Nile and pillaged along the frontier of the kingdom of Maqurra, which by the seventh century had absorbed the state of Nobatia. Raid and counterraid between the Arabs and the Nubians followed until a well equipped Arab expedition under Abd Allah ibn Sad ibn Abi Sarh was sent south to punish the Nubians. The Arabs marched as far as Dunqula, laid siege to the town, and destroyed the Christian cathedral. They suffered heavy casualties, however, so that when the king of Maqurra sought an armistice, Abd Allah ibn Sad agreed to peace, happy to extricate his battered forces from a precarious position. Arab-Nubian relations were subsequently regularized by an annual exchange of gifts, trade relations, and the mutual understanding that no Muslims were to settle in Nubia and no Nubians were to take up residence in Egypt. With but few interruptions this peaceful, commercial relationship lasted for nearly six centuries, its very success undoubtedly the result of the mutual interest which both the Arabs and the Nubians derived from it. The Arabs received a stable frontier. They appear to have had no designs to occupy the Sudan and were probably discouraged from doing so by the arid plains beside the Aswan Reach. Peace on the frontier was their object, and this the treaty guaranteed. In return the kingdom of Maqurra received another six hundred years of life.

So long as the Arabs ruled Egypt, peace was maintained on the Nubian frontier, but when non-Arabs acquired control of the delta, friction arose in Upper Egypt. In the ninth century the Tulunid rulers of Egypt urged the nomadic Arab tribes to follow the Nile southward in order to eliminate such unruly and troublesome subjects from their midst. Lured by the prospects of gold in the Nubian desert, the nomads pressed into Nubia, raiding and pillaging along the borders, but the heartland of Maqurra remained free from direct hostilities until the Mamluks established their control over Egypt. In the late thirteenth and early fourteenth centuries the Mamluk sultans sent regular military expeditions against Maqurra, as much to rid Egypt of uncontrollable Arab beduins as to capture Nubia.

The Mamluks never succeeded in actually occupying Maqurra, but they devastated the country, draining its political and economic vitality and plunging it into chaos and depression. By the fifteenth century Dunqula was no longer strong enough to withstand Arab encroachment, and the country was open to Arab immigration. Once the Arab nomads, particularly the Juhayna, learned that the land beyond the Aswan Reach could support their herds and that no political authority had the power to turn them back, they began to migrate southward, intermarrying with the Nubians and introducing Arabic, Muslim culture to the Christian inhabitants. The patrilineal Arabs soon acquired control from the matrilineal Nubians, since intermarriage resulted in Nubian inheritance passing from Nubian women to their half-Arab sons, but the Arabs replaced political authority in Maqurra only with their own nomadic tribal institutions. And so from Dunqula the Juhayna and others wandered east and west of the Nile with their herds, for to the south the kingdom of Alwa remained intact as the last indigenous Christian barrier to the Arab occupation of the Sudan.

Alwa extended from Kabushiyya as far south as Sennar. Beyond, from the Ethiopian escarpment to the White Nile lived Nilotic peoples about which little is known. Alwa appears to have been much more prosperous and stronger than Maqurra. It had preserved the ironworking techniques of Kush, and its capital at Suba possessed many impressive buildings, churches, and gardens. Christianity remained the state religion, but its long isolation from the Christian world had probably resulted in bizarre and syncretistic accretions to liturgy and ritual. Alwa was able to maintain its integrity so long as the Arabs failed to combine against it, but the continuous and corrosive raids of the beduins throughout the fifteenth century clearly weakened its power to resist. Thus, when an Arab confederation led by Abd Allah Jamma was at last brought together to assault the Christian kingdom, Alwa collapsed. Suba and the Blue Nile region were abandoned, left to the Funj, who suddenly appeared, seemingly from nowhere, to establish their authority from Sennar to the main Nile.

The Funj were a strange and mysterious people. All that is known of their origins is the fact that they were neither Arabs nor Muslims.[22] Under their leader, Amara Dunqas, the Funj founded their

[22] For a summary of the controversy see P. M. Holt, "Funj Origins: A Critique and New Evidence," *Journal of African History*, IV, No. 1 (1963), 39-55.

capital at Sennar and throughout the sixteenth century struggled for control of the Gezira region against the Arab tribes who had settled around the confluence of the Blue and the White Niles. The Funj appear to have firmly established their supremacy by 1607-8. By the mid-seventeenth century the Funj dynasty had reached its golden age under one of their greatest kings, Badi II Abu Daqn (1644/45-1680), who extended Funj suzerainty across the White Nile into Kordofan and reduced the tribal chieftaincies scattered northward along the main Nile to tribute-paying feudatories. But as Badi expanded Funj power, he also planted the seeds of Funj decline. During his conquests slaves were captured and taken to Sennar, where, as they grew in numbers and influence, they formed a slave army, not unlike the Janizaries of the Ottoman Empire. Loyal to the monarch alone, the slaves soon came to compete with the Funj aristocracy for control of the offices of state. Intrigue and hostility between these two rival groups soon led to open rebellion which undermined the position of the traditional ruling class. Under Badi IV Abu Shulukh (1724-62) the ruling aristocracy was finally broken, and the king assumed arbitrary power, supported by his slave troops. So long as Badi IV could command the loyalty of his army, his position was secure and the kingdom enjoyed a respite from internal strife, but at the end of his long reign control of the army slipped from the aged Badi. Under the leadership of his viceroy in Kordofan, Abu Likaylik, the army turned against the king and banished him to exile at Suba. Abu Likaylik was of Hamaj origins, and his emergence probably represented a resurgence of older indigenous elements who had been Arabized and Islamized but were neither Arab nor Funj. Henceforward the Funj kings were but puppets of the viziers, whose struggles to win and to keep control precipitated the kingdom into steady decline, interrupted only by infrequent periods of peace and stability established by a strong vizier who was able to overcome his rivals. During its last half century the Funj kingdom was a spent state, kept intact only through want of a rival but gradually disintegrating through wars, intrigue, and conspiracy, until the forces of Muhammad Ali advanced on Sennar in 1821 and pushed the Funj empire into oblivion.

The Funj were originally pagans, but the aristocracy soon adopted Islam and, although they retained many pagan customs, remained nominal Muslims. The conversion was largely the work of a handful of Islamic missionaries, holy men, who came to the Sudan from the

larger Muslim world. The great success of these missionaries, however, was not among the Funj but among the riverine population of
Arabized Nubians. Among these villagers the missionaries instilled
a deep devotion to Islam which appears to have been conspicuously
absent among the nomad Arabs who first reached the Sudan after the
collapse of the kingdom of Maqurra. These few intrepid missionaries
were, for the most part, teachers who had studied in Egypt or the
Hijaz and who came to the Sudan to impart a knowledge of holy law
and instruction in the proper forms of Islamic piety and worship. The
earliest such missionary was Ghulamallah ibn Aid from the Yemen,
who settled at Dunqula in the fourteenth century. He was followed
in the fifteenth century by Hamad Abu Dunana who, although like
Ghulamallah claimed to be descended from the Prophet, appears to
have emphasized the way to God through the mystical exercises of
Sufism rather than through the more orthodox interpretations of the
Koran taught by Ghulamallah.

Despite the lasting-work of Ghulamallah and Abu Dunana, missionary work in the Sudan remained a frustrating if not hazardous
undertaking until the sixteenth century, when the collapse of the
Christian kingdom of Alwa was complete and the hegemony of the
Funj enhanced security. Under the inspiration of Mahmud al-Araki,
a Sudanese who had studied in Egypt, numerous schools of religious
learning were founded along the White Nile in the sixteenth and
seventeenth centuries, while in the middle of the sixteenth century
Ibrahim al-Bulad proselytized among the Shayqiyya. Like al-Araki,
al-Bulad studied in Egypt and then returned to the Sudan, where he
taught law and introduced two standard texts which remain today
the foundation of Muslim legal learning in the Sudan, *al-Risala* of
Ibn Abi Zayd al-Qayrawani and *al-Mukhtasar* of Khalil ibn Ishaq,
known commonly as the Khalil. Both these men were jurists who
taught the law, but many of the more famous Sudanese holy men
who followed them were Sufi missionaries, members of the influential
religious brotherhoods who sought the way to God through religious
mysticism, not legal texts. One of them, Hamad ibn Muhammad
al-Majdhub founded a celebrated family of holy men, the Majadhib,
in the eighteenth century. His grandson Muhammad al-Majdhub,
al-faki al-kabir (the great teacher), continued the tradition from
the family seat of learning at Al Damir. Although the fervor
of Sudanese Islam waned in the eighteenth century, the great religious reform movements which shook the Muslim world in the late

eighteenth and early nineteenth centuries produced a revivalist spirit among the Sufi orders in the Sudan. Out of that revivalism was born a new order, the Mirghaniyya or Khatmiyya, later to become one of the strongest in the modern Sudan.

By the time of the Turko-Egyptian conquest Sudanese Islam had thus been invigorated by a tradition of Muslim missionary activity. Not only did these missionaries attract a following by their teachings and piety, but they laid the foundations for a long line of indigenous Sudanese holy men who passed on the way to God taught them by their masters, or who founded their own religious schools, or who, if extraordinarily successful, gathered their own following into a religious order. These *fakis* (from *fiqh*, jurist), as they are called, were at worst parasites on the community who fed off the superstitions of the Sudanese, at best erudite teachers of wide respect who attracted students from all over the Sudan. As teachers and as Sufi mystics the *fakis* held a religious monopoly until the introduction, after Muhammad Ali's conquest, of an official hierarchy of jurists and scholars, the *ulama,* whose orthodox, legalistic conception of Islam was as alien to the Sudanese as were their origins. This disparity between the mystical, traditional *fakis,* close to the Sudanese, if not of them, and the orthodox, Islamic jurists, aloof, if not actually part of the government bureaucracy, created a rivalry which in the past has produced open hostility in times of trouble and sullen suspicion in times of peace. Today, this schism has diminished; the *faki* continues his customary practices unmolested, while the Sudanese have acknowledged the position of the *ulama* in society.

The influence of the *fakis* was not, however, confined solely to religion. Under their guidance Islam regulated the social, political, and ascetic life of the Sudanese, so that the successful *faki* not only controlled the hearts of his followers but commanded their services as well. Endowed with lands and herds, the *faki* increased his influence by wealth as well as by wisdom and not infrequently wielded secular power in addition to spiritual advice. Many of these teachers formed influential dynasties. The *faki* strengthened the traditional, authoritarian concept of society, for just as his secular counterparts, the village headman and the nomad tribal *shaykh,* conducted temporal affairs by authoritarian means, so too the *faki* demanded, as a necessary requirement of the religious brotherhood, absolute acknowledgment of his authority. Thus, at the time of the Turko-Egyptian conquest the Sudanese were equipped to meet the century and a half of upheaval which followed with a profound belief and respect for authority, implanted by religious and secular authoritarianism appealing to their deepest spiritual emotions and governing their political and social consciousness. In spite of the impact of Western technology and education, this respect for authority remains a vital force among the Sudanese today and still conditions their actions and attitudes toward their own domestic problems and those of the world about them.

At the end of the eighteenth century Egypt and the Sudan stood on the threshold of the modern world, each with a distinctive past but possessing certain common characteristics, not the least of which were the elemental waters of the Nile. Both lands contained a mass of peasant cultivators struggling to survive by tilling the narrow belt of arable soil beside the river with their traditional technology. Beyond the Nile in Upper Egypt and on the plains of the Sudan lived beduins, independent nomads who plundered and traded with the settled agricultural communities. Islam was pervasive, if not everywhere acknowledged in the Sudan, and although itself divided into rival factions, the universality of the Islamic community provided a common denominator to bind the diverse peoples of the middle and lower Nile Valley. Arabic and Arab culture had accompanied, or even preceded Islam, but its cultural heritage was circumscribed in the Sudan by a host of local customs and pre-Islamic traditions and diluted in Egypt by non-Arab minorities and ruling elites. Equipped with a common but primitive technology, a common but factious religion, and a common but compromised cultural heritage, Egypt and the Sudan appeared ill-prepared to meet the onrush of modernization.

THREE

THE BEGINNINGS OF MODERNIZATION

Egypt, 1798–1875

Despite the enormous variations in Egyptian history before 1800 there were several basic patterns common to this entire period. The vast majority of the population lived on the land, producing subsistence crops. Extended family and village organizations remained rather self-contained and supported the relative isolation of individual social units within Egypt. The more developed institutions of the central government, economic system, and religious organization were staffed by only a small fraction of Egypt's population and were able to extract from the village-kin organizations only an inconsiderable proportion of the country's resources. In the modern period this rural isolation and self-sufficiency were undermined, and the centralized institutions of government, economic system, religion, and education assumed a dominant role in the lives of the Egyptian people. The beginnings of this transformation occurred in the first three-quarters of the nineteenth century.

The decisive event in Egyptian history was the French invasion in 1798. By conquering Egypt the French sought to straddle a route to the East and threaten Britain's Indian empire as part of the wider Anglo-French conflict. At the same time, France hoped to encourage economic interests in the Middle East, for French merchants looked upon this area as a potential market for their manufactures. By 1798 there were already sixty-one Frenchmen residing in Egypt. Led by the young and ambitious Napoleon Bonaparte, the invasion force was not composed exclusively of soldiers but contained some of the finest French scholars of the age, including engineers, hydraulic experts, agriculturalists, historians, linguists, experts in tropical medicine, Arabists, and others. These experts were expected to advise the French administration of conquered Egypt and to make it profitable to France.

Despite plans for a more or less permanent occupation, the French were overwhelmed by unforeseen difficulties and remained for only a few years. The British Admiral Lord Nelson destroyed the French fleet at Abukir off the Egyptian coast, cutting communications with the European Continent and isolating the French army in Egypt. In Egypt itself the French troops were more successful. With their superior military technology they destroyed their armed opponents, the Mamluks, hacking them to pieces at the Battle of the Pyramids. But the rest of the Egyptian environment proved more forbidding. Napoleon's efforts to show his sympathies for Islam, in dress and proclamation, were futile. The Egyptian people were hostile to the French, and sporadic clashes between the Egyptians and French troops continued. Even more destructive were the diseases. Eye disorders swept through the army and later during the Syrian campaigns the French troops were ravaged by the plague. No longer the invincible military machine that Napoleon had brought to Egypt, the French army was unable to crush a force of Ottoman and English troops in Syria and was confined to Egypt. Frustrated in Egypt, Napoleon abruptly abandoned his troops and returned to France in 1800 to seek military victories and political successes in Europe. In Egypt the fighting and negotiating dragged on for another few years before an agreement was reached permitting the evacuation of French troops.

The immediate impact of the French occupation was the decisive defeat of the Mamluks. The Mamluk regime had been founded on military prowess and depended on military success for its continuation. Thus, defeat brought discredit, and although the Mamluks were able to vie for power after the French withdrawal, the new forms of French military technology and organization rendered their institutions obsolete. But Napoleon had intended a more thoroughgoing transformation of Egypt than simply the defeat of the Mamluks, and the scholars he brought with him carried on investigations which, although of little contemporary importance, had in the long run a profound impact on the course of Egyptian history. These men set to work investigating Egypt's irrigation system and agricultural potentiality. They created an *Institut*, where they gave demonstrations of Western science to Egyptian scholars. Surveying experts studied a project for piercing the Isthmus at Suez but came to the mistaken conclusion that the Red Sea and Mediterranean were at different levels and that a canal would require a series of expensive locks. The fresh water canal running from the Nile to Alexandria was cleared of silt. Plans for a reform of the land taxation system were drawn up. Most of these projects were, of course, never implemented by the French, and in the final analysis, it seems clear that the French impact upon the domestic institutions of Egypt was slight. The occupation was short and troubled. There was only one period of relative calm, when Napoleon had left the country, and this lasted but a year.

The most enduring monument of the French invasion was nonetheless produced by the French scholars who had gone to Egypt. This was the lavish work in many volumes entitled *Description de l'Egypte*. The volumes on ancient Egypt provided much new information on the Pharaonic heritage. Equally impressive, and of great use to scholars ever since, were the four volumes describing Egypt in 1800 (*Description de l'Egypte: Etat Moderne*). The French scholars were shocked by the backwardness of a country which had once been a center of civilization and a great Islamic state. They found a land sparsely populated; their estimate was two and one-half million inhabitants. The hydraulic system on which agricultural productivity depended was in a dreadful state of repair. Canals were poorly aligned and filled with silt. Nor had the Egyptians learned to construct effective dams across the Nile or its canals for raising irrigation water to the soil. Artisan activity was not highly developed. In the larger cities and villages the crafts were limited to pottery, textiles, brickwork, straw mats, sugar, rose water, and salt. There was little trade between villages and little trade outside the country. The French were also appalled by the inadequate sanitary conditions. There were few doctors, and their knowledge was not as precise as that of their European counterparts. In fact, most of the medical work was done by sanitary barbers whose techniques and knowledge the French harshly criticized. The people lived in conditions that provided little protection against the spread of disease. Most villages had no system for the removal of refuse. Modern water supply was unknown; most Egyptians took their water from the Nile or from polluted canals. Even discounting ethnocentric exaggeration, the French scholars described a country which had markedly declined from previous periods of greater technological, economic, and social creativity.

The political vacuum created by the departure of the French was soon filled by the remarkable Muhammad Ali (1805-48), who during his reign began the forced modernization of a traditional society. This period has not received proper attention in comparative studies of modernizing societies, presumably because Muhammad Ali's efforts were not crowned with the success of Stalin's Russia, Tokugawa Japan, or Kemal Ataturk's Turkey. Why this military adventurer, untutored and apparently illiterate, should have been such a keen exponent of modernization remains something of a mystery. Of course, the climate of the age was alive to programs of change, and Muhammad Ali had probably been influenced by the rather abortive efforts to reform the Ottoman army in the latter part of the eighteenth century. In Egypt he certainly must have been impressed with the French defeat of the vaunted Mamluks. French military power, and also that of the English whom he later encountered, must have convinced him of the superiority of Western military technology. Nevertheless, this exposure to Western influence hardly explains his extraordinary efforts to alter so many aspects of Egyptian society.

Muhammad Ali was sent to Egypt by the Ottomans during the French invasion. Upon the withdrawal of French troops he engaged in a three-cornered power struggle with the official representative of the Ottoman empire and the Egyptian Mamluks. In 1805 he was recognized as the viceroy of Egypt by the Ottoman sultan and set about to destroy the influence of the remaining Mamluks. In 1811 he administered the *coup de grâce*. Having invited the Mamluks to negotiations in Cairo, he promptly slaughtered those who had come to a banquet in their honor. Muhammad Ali was now master in Egypt. His strong, unrivaled position facilitated the implementation of energetic programs of social change, whereas many other modernizing leaders encountered irresistible opposition. In the Ottoman empire, for instance, traditional groups, especially the Janizaries until their dissolution, resisted all programs of military modernization. In Egypt Muhammad Ali had eliminated both the Ottoman Janizaries and the Mamluks in his quest for power. He slowly purged his own ranks of those individuals who might have opposed him, and, at the same time, he rewarded those loyal to the regime with lands and political offices. The only group capable of opposition were the *ulama*. Some, in fact, did resist, but on the whole the *ulama* did not concern themselves greatly with political affairs as long as their dominance in religious matters was not threatened. Moreover, Muhammad Ali astutely employed *ulama* in some of his new educational institutions.

The linchpin of Muhammad Ali's programs of modernization was military reform. In this his reforms were much like those of the Ottoman sultan of the period and of other early modernizers of backward societies. This has sometimes been called defensive modernization, and the viceroy's goal was certainly to redress the balance of power between Egypt and Europe. In this effort he inevitably looked to Europe for technical assistance, Egypt having no personnel trained in European military techniques. At first he relied upon Italians and dispatched his earliest missions to Italy. Dissatisfied with their training, he then turned to France. His overtures were met with ready acceptance both by the French government and by private French citizens. After 1810 a French military mission under General Boyer was sent to Egypt to advise on military changes, and a host of French technicians soon followed. Most of these men were not official representatives of the French government; some, men like Colonel Seve (later Sulayman Pasha in Egypt), had fought in the Napoleonic campaigns and after 1815 felt dissatisfied in a less militaristic French society. Indeed, French officials became influential in virtually every important area of Egyptian modernization: Colonel Seve in the army, de Cerisy in shipbuilding, Clot Bey and Perron at the medical school, Jumel, the hydraulic engineer and developer of the new Egyptian cotton plant, Linant de Bellefonds and Mougel as irrigation experts. At the same time Muhammad Ali also dispatched many educational missions to France so that Egyptian students could pursue higher studies in medicine, engineering, warfare, and other technical subjects. To be sure, the viceroy tried to diversify his borrowing. He brought in technical experts from other countries and also sent educational missions to other states, but the French clearly dominated the modernization program in Egypt during this period.

Muhammad Ali's goal was to transform Egypt into the most powerful military state in the Middle East and to acquire for himself and his family full-fledged recognition of the right to rule over Egypt and any conquered territories. The first modern schools opened in Egypt were for military training. Military technicians were brought to Egypt to teach in these schools and to reorganize the armed forces. The upper ranks of the army were mainly staffed by Europeans and by Turks, but the rank and file had to be drawn from other sources. Muhammad Ali hoped through the conquest of the

Sudan to find a source of recruits there. The Sudanese, however, did not thrive well in the Egyptian climate, and ultimately the viceroy began conscripting Egyptian peasants. The peasants found the new military leaders very harsh taskmasters, and so many able-bodied males were recruited into the army that the fields were often tilled by old men, women, and children. Military levies were dreaded, and many peasants attempted to flee their villages, only to be forcibly returned to their lands by the state.

Muhammad Ali was shrewd enough to realize that military modernization was not sufficient. Economic strength, educational reform, sanitary improvement, and many other changes were required to support military technology. In many instances the first efforts to effect change in these nonmilitary areas were carried out under the auspices of the armed forces, but in time many programs obtained a life of their own and were able to exist independent of military considerations. An examination of educational reform and public health will illustrate these points.

The educational program was closely wedded to military modernization in the early part of Muhammad Ali's reign. The department of education was a branch of the war ministry, and the first modern schools were military academies. But the country's needs required a diversification of the educational system. Doctors, engineers, translators, civil servants were needed for army and administration. Westernized primary and secondary schools were created, and once these schools began to send forth graduates, higher schools and colleges were required. Schools of medicine, veterinary science, engineering, and translation were thus established, but not all of their graduates were absorbed into the military bureaucracy.

The beginnings of modern public health reform in Egypt may be found in the extraordinary career of A. B. Clot Bey. A young French physician and scholar, he was persuaded to come to Egypt in the 1820s to head a medical program for the army. His early work was almost exclusively devoted to protecting the health of the Egyptian army, but Clot was a man of ambition and imagination who desired to make a more profound impact on the transformation of Egypt than he could as an army doctor. He persuaded the viceroy to allow him to create a medical school in Egypt. Other educational experiments followed. A school of veterinary science was established, as well as a school of midwifery. Under Clot's guidance the school of medicine at Abuzabel became one of Egypt's most creative institutions of social change. Over protests from conservative *ulama* he set up a course in human anatomy for his students and performed surgical experiments on the human body. The school became an important center for the translation into Arabic and Turkish of works on medicine and science in European languages. Some of Egypt's most creative intellectuals, including Rifaa al-Tahtawi, were associated with the school, and the institution counted among its teaching staff the only European with real fluency in Arabic, Dr. Perron, who was chiefly responsible for the school's outstanding translation achievements.

Even a cursory glance at Muhammad Ali's programs suggests the crucial importance of translations from European languages of all the lectures and books used in courses. Muhammad Ali was in the habit of ordering students returning from Europe to provide him with translations of all the books they had used in their studies. In time, a school of languages was created by Rifaa al-Tahtawi for the express purpose of turning out men who could cope with the tremendous problems of translation. The graduates of this school translated many European books required by the schools in Egypt and served as translators of lectures given by Europeans in the Egyptian schools. The difficulties of attempting to borrow European science through the medium of translated works can well be imagined. In the early years of Muhammad Ali's reign there were only a few men qualified in Arabic or Turkish and a European language. Most of these early translators were Syrian Christians who had been able to learn a European language through their missionary contacts. It would have been asking too much of these very talented men, however, to be equally skilled in the scientific terminology they were translating. Consequently, most of their translations of European scientific works were far from precise and misled students as often as they helped them.

The classroom problems were also staggering. European teachers who knew no Arabic gave lectures in their own languages. These were translated simultaneously for the students, and student questions had once again to be translated to the teacher. A survey conducted in the 1830s by an Egyptian committee showed that this system was unsatisfactory, resulting in frequent breakdowns of communication between teachers and students. The inadequacy of Arabic for modern scientific terminology was an incredible obstacle. Translators had either to search in the classical Arabic language for a word with an approximate meaning or else had to Arabize the European word. Since each translator did very much as he pleased and the practice of putting the European word in brackets was uncommon, further difficulties were created for defenseless students. The establishment of the school of languages helped to lessen some of these problems. Rules evolved for translating, and a new vocabulary gradually came into existence. Moreover, the custom of employing correctors and editors to check over translated manuscripts and lectures immensely improved the caliber and clarity of translations.

Of course, the problems of borrowing European science were not peculiar to Egypt, but the Egyptian experience illustrates the language problems common to developing countries. Since the Middle East did not participate in Europe's scientific and technological revolutions, its languages did not have a vocabulary corresponding to European scientific terminology. As long as European languages were not widespread among the educated people, the language of instruction in the higher schools had to be Arabic. At the same time, European languages were introduced into the lower schools so that instruction in these languages would eventually be possible in the higher schools. Thus, a dual effort was made to overcome the language problem: on the one hand, the modernization of Arabic, on the other, the introduction and spread of European languages.

Egypt's military modernization depended upon its economic resources, and only by increasing the wealth of the country and the revenues of the state could Muhammad Ali afford his expensive programs. The key to economic development was the introduction of perennial irrigation and the cultivation of a new cash crop, cotton. In order to maximize state revenues Muhammad Ali introduced the monopoly system into agriculture, by which the state monopolized the purchase of key agricultural products, paying low prices to the peasant farmer and selling the products either in Egypt or to foreign merchants at much higher prices. These exploitative practices were deeply resented both by the Egyptian peasantry, who continued to live at appallingly low levels of subsistence, and by European merchants, who were forced to pay high prices for their goods. The peasants were incapable of altering the system, but the merchants were more powerful, and in the last years of Muhammad Ali's reign they forced the state to renounce its monopolistic restrictions.

The most ambitious aspect of Muhammad Ali's modernization was his program of industrialization. Behind this drive were the same military considerations, for the viceroy wanted to make his armed forces and economic system less dependent on Europe. Once again technicians were imported from Europe. Steel foundries were established at Bulaq, and an arsenal and shipbuilding plant founded at Alexandria. Woolen factories, a sugar refining factory, glass and gunpowder mills were also established. The most important development was the creation of a cotton industry. By 1828 one quarter of the cotton grown in Egypt was consumed in its factories. In 1837 twenty-nine Egyptian factories produced fifty thousand kantars of yarn. In general, the factories were run at a considerable loss to the state. Steam power was scarce, and most of the machinery was driven by animals. There was an inadequate stock of spare parts, and a lack of engineers to repair broken machinery. These difficulties alone would probably have precipitated the collapse of these early efforts at industrialization. But when the foreign merchants succeeded in reducing tariffs and curtailing the monopolistic powers by which Muhammad Ali had protected national industries, Egyptian industry was destroyed. Once European merchants were free to sell European manufactures in Egypt, local industry could not compete with the lower priced European goods.

Since the reform programs were so heavily geared to military considerations, their ultimate success or failure depended upon the fortunes of Egyptian military campaigns. At first Muhammad Ali's forces swept all before them. In 1812 the Egyptian army, just at the beginning of its transformation, drove Wahhabi forces from the holy places in the Arabian peninsula. This campaign was waged by the Egyptian army acting as an agent of the Ottoman empire, which they were also to serve during the Greek War of Independence. Both the Egyptian army and a newly constructed Egyptian naval squadron were sent to put down the Greek insurgents. Although the troops fought with great effectiveness, European intervention on the side of the Greeks nullified their efforts, and most of the Egyptian fleet was sunk in the Bay of Navarino by a combined force of English, French, and Russian vessels.

Muhammad Ali fought these two campaigns on the side of the Ottoman empire for the purpose of winning political independence for his regime in Egypt. But at the same time, the Ottoman sultans sought to reassert their authority over the increasingly independent attitude of their viceroy in Egypt. In the 1830s these tensions erupted into open war, first between 1831 and 1833, then again in 1839-

40. Had the wars been fought in isolation from European diplomacy, the outcome would never have been in doubt. Muhammad Ali's programs of modernization had gone much further than Ottoman reforms, and the Ottoman army was no match for Egyptian troops. On both occasions the Egyptian army drove through Syria and into Turkey. The way to Constantinople lay open, and but for the intervention of the European powers, Muhammad Ali might have made himself ruler of the Ottoman empire. Britain and Russia were particularly alarmed by Egyptian success against the Ottomans; the British because they were concerned about the routes to India, the Russians because of their desire to expand into the Ottoman empire from the north. In the crisis of 1840 the combined strength of all the European powers but France were marshaled against Egypt. The Egyptian army was defeated by European troops, and although Muhammad Ali received sympathy from Paris, he acquired no tangible support and was forced to conclude peace with the Ottomans. The treaty was a crushing blow to the viceroy. Although recognizing the rights of Muhammad Ali to rule Egypt, the treaty limited the size of the Egyptian army and broke the viceroy's monopolistic commercial and agricultural powers.

The destruction of Muhammad Ali's ambitious hopes symbolized by the treaty limitation of the army cooled the aging viceroy's enthusiasm for modernization. The motives for transforming Egyptian society no longer applied, and from 1840 until Muhammad Ali's death a whole host of reform projects were allowed to languish. Many of the modern schools were closed; fewer educational missions were sent to Europe; the pace of translation of foreign books slackened. In sum, Egypt's modernization was blunted once the military ambitions of its ruler had been thwarted.

The immediate successors to Muhammad Ali—Abbas (1848-54) and Said (1854-63)—were not cut from the same cloth as their predecessor. Although Abbas is credited with the construction of Egypt's first railroad, he has been described as a reactionary who reversed the modernizing trends in Egypt. Said was a colorless figure, and his chief claim to recognition is that he gave Ferdinand de Lesseps the concessions to construct the Suez Canal. These two figures pale even more in comparison with the controversial, flamboyant Ismail, ruler of Egypt from 1863 until his deposition in 1879.

Ismail was European-educated. Like Muhammad Ali, he was committed to modernization, but for him military considerations were not paramount. Ismail certainly wanted to strengthen his state and the position of the ruling family in the state, but he was equally interested in Europeanizing his country and was fond of remarking that Egypt was becoming an extension of European civilization. He expanded the educational system and sent educational missions to Europe. Moreover, he sought to modernize and to beautify the cities of Egypt and to encourage European culture. An opera house was built in Cairo, and there the premiere of Verdi's *Aida* was performed in 1869 for the opening of the Suez Canal. Newspapers flourished, although their attacks upon his regime ultimately became a source of discomfort to him. A consultative assembly was created in the 1860s in imitation of European parliamentary bodies. The beautification of Egypt's major cities was, indeed, one of the most notable developments of this era. Cairo was rebuilt in imitation of Baron Hausmann's modernization of Paris. New wide boulevards were cut through the city. Gardens and parks were created. Gas lighting was provided on the streets of the wealthier sections of the city. The French influence on Cairo's development remains unmistakable to this day.

The feverish pace of these activities should not obscure their lack of social content. Ismail did not intend any major social revolution by his reform programs, and those social alterations that took place and were to culminate in the Arabi revolt (1879-82) were not foreseen by him. Ismail wanted Egypt to be a land of refinement and sophistication, respected and praised by Europeans. He even purchased the more exalted title, khedive, from the Ottoman sultan. But he had no intention of rooting out poverty, improving the lot of the peasant, or equalizing the distribution of wealth. On several occasions while he was passing along one of the new lovely boulevards of Cairo, Ismail's eye was caught by areas of filth and squalor that marred the beauty of the ride. His response was to order high walls to be built around these areas so that they would not disturb the passerby. Under Ismail, Egypt's upper classes flourished. The major cities became more cosmopolitan as Europeans came to regard Egypt as part of the "civilized" world, but the lot of the lower classes remained much as it had been before.

The economic foundations for Ismail's modernization rested on two sources: the export of cotton and the borrowing of capital. In Ismail's reign cotton came to dominate the export economy, for during the American Civil War the American South was blockaded and unable to send cotton to the great textile producers of Europe. They looked to other sources, and in Egypt the price of cotton dramatically increased and the crop soon occupied an unchallenged position in the country's economy.

Capital borrowing had commenced under Ismail's predecessor, Said, but reached astonishing heights under Ismail. Said bequeathed to Ismail a small foreign debt; Ismail at his deposition in 1879 had increased this debt to £100 million and had driven Egypt into bankruptcy. Three factors accounted for this. The first was the aggressiveness of European capitalists in Egypt. Europeans enjoyed a most favorable position in Egypt through their capitulatory privileges acquired since the sixteenth century which gave them inviolability of domicile, exemption from Egyptian laws except by the consent of their governments, and most especially the right to have all legal matters, criminal and civil, tried in their own consular courts.[1] The European financiers who were attracted to Egypt comprised a particularly aggressive group on the fringe of the more conservative financial interests in Europe. This group had first manifested its influence by successfully resisting Muhammad Ali's system of commercial and agricultural monopolies. They were interested in quick and high profits gained by exploitation, not in the country's orderly and rational development. With the support of their own consular courts they were able to use the Egyptian government for their own advantage and to win large financial concessions for themselves.

The second reason was the unfavorable terms under which Ismail contracted many of his loans in Europe. As his financial plight became more desperate and his needs for money greater, he borrowed at crushing rates of interest. Perhaps his most disastrous financial bargain arose over a dispute with Ferdinand de Lesseps' Suez Canal Company. According to the concession granted by Said to de Lesseps, Egypt was to provide labor to dig the canal and to cede certain lands bordering on the waterway. These obligations proved onerous to Ismail, for he was in the midst of the cotton boom and did not want a large part of his labor force called away for work on the canal. Moreover, he feared that the cession of land to the Canal Company would make the company a virtual state within a state. The khedive set about to rescind these concessions, and eventually he agreed to submit his dispute with the Canal Company to Napoleon III,

[1] Civil cases were taken out of the hands of consular courts and given to new judicial bodies, the Mixed Tribunals, in 1875.

Emperor of France. A more partisan arbitrator could not have been found, for the Canal Company was a private French company. Not surprisingly, Napoleon decided that the Egyptian government should pay the Canal Company an indemnity of eighty-four million francs for the rescinding of these concessions, a sum that went a long way toward easing the company's financial burdens but which placed Ismail heavily in debt at the very outset of his reign.

European capitalists alone cannot be blamed for Egypt's dismal financial plight. The third factor was khedivial extravagance. To be sure, a great deal of the money was spent on worthwhile programs of modernization—schools, educational missions, canals, railroads, and other projects—but money was also spent on such showpieces as the new opera house, magnificent palaces, and the sumptuous entertainment provided for European royalty at the opening of the Suez Canal. Extraordinary amounts of money were sent to the Ottoman empire, in the form of bribes, tribute, and gifts, in order to strengthen the position of the ruling family in Egypt. By 1875 Egypt was on the verge of bankruptcy. Egyptian credit had been exhausted in Europe, and to stave off one financial crisis the khedive sold Egyptian government shares in the Suez Canal Company to the British for £4,000,000. Already a large part of Egyptian assets had been pledged to European creditors, including customs revenue, receipts from railways, and profits from the private estates of the khedive. Finally, in desperation Ismail requested a European financial adviser to be sent to Cairo to resolve the problem of Egyptian finances. The British sent Stephen Cave in 1875. In the following year Ismail was compelled to create an international body, known as the *Caisse de la Dette Publique,* which represented those European powers with important financial interests in Egypt and received payments on Egypt's foreign debt. A British and a French official were appointed as "advisers" to the Egyptian ministries of finance and public works, the two most powerful administrative branches. The era of Egyptian political independence and defensive modernization was drawing to a close. Pressures from the European financial community were gradually being transformed into the imposition of foreign political controls over Egypt.

The construction and opening of the Suez Canal typifies much in Ismail's reign: financial extravagance, involvement in European diplomacy, exploitation of the Egyptian peasantry, and desire to impress Europe with the high level of civilization in Egypt. Actually, the original concessions were wrung by Ferdinand de Lesseps from Ismail's predecessor, Said. They were far-reaching, for they gave the Canal Company the rights to operate the canal for a period of ninety-nine years from its opening. Moreover, Said agreed to provide Egyptian labor for canal construction, and until Napoleon III's indemnity agreement with Ismail Egyptian peasants were forcibly recruited as laborers for the Canal Company. Ironically, although Egypt provided large labor forces and a great deal of the financing for the canal, it derived almost no financial return after Ismail sold his shares in the company to the British in 1875. The rather meager concessions made by the Canal Company to Egypt in the twentieth century did not alter the injustice of this situation, and the canal was always regarded with bitterness by Egyptian nationalists as a symbol of exploitative European imperialism.

The construction of the Suez Canal altered Egyptian history in many ways. In purely physical terms it resulted in the creation of two new canal cities, Port Said and Ismailia, where once there had been only desert. The city of Suez, which had previously existed, enjoyed a period of expansion and prosperity. Before the opening of the canal Egypt had been an important entrepot between East and West, but almost immediately afterward Egypt became the primary sea route to India, Australia, and the Orient. British shipping soon came to dominate the use of the canal. British diplomats had originally opposed the construction of the canal, fearing French domination of Egypt and the route to the East and quite rightly realizing that the presence of a canal in Egypt must alter Britain's relationship to that country. The opening of the canal stimulated Britain's interests in Egypt, for the British could ill afford to have any hostile power controlling this important waterway. Even before the occupation of 1882 there was considerable debate in England on the issue of establishing British predominance in Egypt, and a group of British journalists called for preemptive action to prevent its control by any other power. The less imperialistic were just as adamant for keeping Egypt independent, and in 1877 William Ewart Gladstone, the leader of the Liberal Party, wrote an article in *Nineteenth Century* arguing that a British occupation would do irremedial harm to Great Britain by committing the country to an African empire and by deflecting its energies to overseas affairs.

Modernization in Egypt during the first three-quarters of the nineteenth century offers certain useful comparisons with other modernizing societies. A late modernizing society has the distinct advantage of studying the experience of its predecessors in order to avoid their mistakes. Thus, an economically primitive society does not encounter the problem of economic obsolescence so familiar to the more developed countries; the factories, technical skills, and knowledge utilized by late modernizers are the most advanced to be found.[2] These late modernizers have had clearer definitions of their goals and have been able to introduce more planning than their predecessors had. In addition, they have been able to borrow capital and technical skills from the early modernizers.

In Egypt the most acute obstacles to modernization were a lack of skilled personnel and a dearth of accumulated capital. The solution to the first problem was obvious: a dual program of importing foreign technicians into Egypt and training Egyptians in foreign schools. Nearly every late modernizing society has followed this solution to the problem of technical expertise. But the second problem, that of providing capital for modernization, has been resolved in different ways by different countries. Some have borrowed capital. Others have mobilized the capital already present within the society through new financial institutions. Others have tried to squeeze capital out of the agrarian economy by strict governmental controls and the imposition of harsh standards of living on the population. In the nineteenth century Egypt employed two different approaches. Under Muhammad Ali modernization was financed by means of a highly developed set of government controls over the rural economy. Peasants were forced to sell their products to the state at low prices, and then the state redistributed these goods abroad and within the country at much higher prices. The revenue garnered from this operation was employed to finance modernization. This system collapsed, in part because of opposition from foreign merchants in Egypt, and Muhammad Ali's successors were increasingly driven to borrowing. In weak states this kind of financial dependence on Europe has contributed to the imposition of European political control, and such was the outcome in Egypt.

One of the most critical consequences of these techniques of modernization was the domination of financial and commercial activities in Egypt by a European middle class. Muhammad Ali had, of course,

[2] Alexander Gerschenkron, *Economic Backwardness in Historical Perspective: A Book of Essays* (Cambridge, Mass.: 1962).

attempted to promote and control Egypt's commercial and industrial development, but even then Europeans were gaining a favored position through their special privileges. Under Ismail the European commercial community became one of the most aggressive agencies for social change in Egypt. European finance was particularly attracted to banking establishments, real estate, the movement of goods for export, transportation, and communication—the modernized sectors of the economy. From this period until the conclusion of the First World War, Egyptians were almost completely excluded from modern commercial and industrial establishments. There were no Egyptian-financed or Egyptian-controlled banks, no Egyptian-run modern industries, few Egyptian land companies.

A second important aspect of modernization was the growth of the power and scope of centralized political, economic, and educational institutions. The isolation of village and kin groups from each other and from centralized institutions was gradually breaking down. In the political sphere the central government interfered more actively in the lives of the people. Peasants were recruited into the army. New public health regulations were applied to them. Many were vaccinated by government health officials. During epidemics the activities of the people were controlled by government quarantine officials. In the economic sphere the most important changes in the direction of centralization were the more widespread use of markets and money and the introduction of cotton. The peasants now produced more than subsistence crops for local consumption. They grew cotton, sold their crops at markets, and purchased products at these markets for their own needs. Perhaps potentially the most far-reaching of the changes were educational reforms. Education had been a concern of kin and village groups, and it had strengthened these local groups at the expense of the central institutions. Thus, when new modernized government schools were founded, part of the socialization of the young was taken out of the hands of family and village communities. This change tended to undermine the authority and respect accorded family and village and established a new source of authority and, quite often, a new set of values.

A third factor was the emergence in Egypt of a new Western-educated elite. These men have been called a "salaried middle class" because they either held or aspired to hold salaried positions in the new modernized institutions of government, education, and the professions.[3] These were the men who had been trained in Egypt's Westernized schools. The elite of this group had graduated from Egypt's professional schools—law, medicine, and engineering—and some had been to Europe for further education. The communality of their goals bound them together. Their Western education and training committed them to further modernization, and, of course, in practical terms modernization meant more salaried jobs, greater prestige for the Western-educated, greater opportunities for them to find fulfillment within Egyptian society. Modernization also accorded with their values, for these educated men were impressed by what they knew of the West. Superficially, they were particularly struck by its military power, but those who had a chance to observe Europe more closely were attracted to its liberal and humanitarian traditions, its democratic institutions, the higher role of women, and the other more positive aspects of European civilization. Although the Western-educated were at first rather dependent upon encouragement from the state, by the end of Ismail's reign they no longer needed its support. Indeed, they were openly critical of the government and were an important factor in bringing about the Arabi revolt against the existing order.

No description of the Egyptian Western-educated class in the first half of the nineteenth century would be complete without mention of its most remarkable figure, Rifaa Badawi Rafi al-Tahtawi (1801-73). The first part of Tahtawi's career was not typical of other Egyptian intellectuals of this period, for he was educated not in the government schools but at al-Azhar, the center of religious conservatism. His teacher, however, was a well read and open-minded man who gave Tahtawi some exposure to the new knowledge being introduced into Egypt. The turning point in his career came when he was sent as *imam* (chaplain) to accompany one of Muhammad Ali's educational missions to Paris. In France he had an unparalleled opportunity to observe European civilization and to converse with European scholars and orientalists. Returning to Egypt, he organized a school of languages and promoted the work of translations from European languages, particularly in the fields of political theory and science. In order to familiarize educated Egyptians with European civilizations, he wrote an account in Arabic of his experiences and impressions in Europe, and he was one of the first Egyptian intel-

[3] Manfred Halpern, *The Politics of Social Change in the Middle East and North Africa* (Princeton: 1963).

lectuals to attempt to reconcile Islam with modern European civilization. In this effort he tried to demonstrate the compatibility between the European values of reason, democracy, and science and some of the teachings of Muhammad. Tahtawi was also an early exponent of Egyptian nationalism and of the introduction of European political institutions.

The Sudan During the Turkiya

In July 1820 a motley army of some four thousand Turks, Albanians, and Magharba volunteers from the Barbary Coast under the command of Ismail Pasha, the youngest son of Muhammad Ali, the viceroy of Egypt, left Cairo to conquer the lands beyond the Aswan Reach.[4] Muhammad Ali had a multitude of reasons for wanting to add the middle Nile Valley to his empire. He required slaves for his army. He needed gold, which the Sudan was reputed to have in abundance, for his schemes of modernization in Egypt. He sought to eliminate the remnants of the Mamluks who had taken refuge at Dunqula after their power in Egypt had been destroyed. Moreover, territory is the essence of empire, and Muhammad Ali sought just such an imperial symbol by the acquisition of the vast hinterland stretching south from Egypt. The army moved triumphantly up the Nile. Only the Shayqiyya offered resistance, but the dauntless courage and long spears of these wild horsemen were no match for the artillery and firearms of the Turks. The Shayqiyya capitulated, enlisted as irregular cavalry in Ismail's army, and thereafter were scattered throughout the Sudan in the Egyptian service. By May 1821 Ismail had reached the junction of the Blue Nile and the White and pressed on to Sennar, where the last of the Funj sultans ignominiously surrendered and was pensioned off into the limbo of history. While Ismail was conquering the riverine Sudan,

---

[4] The terms *Egyptian* and *Turk* are employed here interchangeably but inaccurately to describe alien rule in the Sudan in the nineteenth century. The invaders and rulers of the Sudan were not Egyptians as we know them today but a Turkish-speaking, multiracial microcosm of the ruling class which had governed Egypt for centuries. Of the twenty-three "Turkish" rulers of the Sudan between 1821 and 1885, eight were Circassians, two Kurds, two Greeks, one Albanian, one Berberine Egyptian, four of unknown origin, and only five actually Turks. See R. L. Hill, *Egypt in the Sudan* (London: 1959), p. 1. To the Sudanese, however, this motley assortment were all called Turks because they spoke Turkish. The period of their rule is known as the Turkiya, but the fact they came from Egypt gives an equal claim to that appellation.

a second army under Muhammad Bey Khusraw, the Daftardar (treasurer), marched south, crushed the levies of the Fur sultan passively awaiting the Egyptians at Bara, and attached Kordofan to the Nilotic conquests of Ismail. The Sudan from Nubia to the Ethiopian foothills and from the Atbara to the Darfur marches was now part of the expanding empire of Muhammad Ali.

Although the conquest of the Sudan was accomplished with surprisingly little bloodshed, its administration was not. Muhammad Ali had acquired the Sudan in order to exploit its human and natural resources, and the demands for taxation which followed amounted to virtual confiscation of gold, livestock, and slaves. It is one thing to reduce a man's standard of living; it is quite another to reduce his political and social position in the community. The extreme taxation of the Turks threatened to do both to the established Sudanese. Everywhere hatred of the Turk became intense, eventually erupting into rebellion and the murder of Ismail and his bodyguard in October 1822 by Nimr, chief of Shandi, and his Jaaliyin followers. From Al Damir to Sennar the Sudanese assaulted Egyptian garrisons, massacring the weaker posts, besieging the stronger ones. The revolt itself was a blind and frustrated protest against the presence and oppression of the Turks. The rebels had no positive goal to unite their hatred nor a single leader to coordinate their attacks. Nor were Sudanese courage and overwhelming numbers a match for the superior firepower of the Egyptian forces. When the army of the Daftardar arrived from Kordofan to suppress the rebellion and avenge Ismail's death, it brushed aside the disorganized Sudanese resistance and moved victoriously along the Nile, destroying villages and slaughtering their inhabitants. By 1824 the revolt was over. All that remained were scores of burnt villages, hundreds of refugees hiding in the hinterland, and a sullen but deep bitterness toward the Turks which was a living memory sixty years later when the Mahdi marched against them.

At first the new government met hostility with repression, and under the leadership of a Circassian, Uthman Bey Jarkas al-Birinji, did little but collect the taxes and brutally crush the slightest resistance. Epidemic, famine, and depopulation were the bitter fruits of this unenlightened policy. In 1825 Ali Khurshid Agha was appointed to replace Uthman at Khartoum, and by 1833 he was in charge of the whole of the Sudan. His administration marked a new era in Egyptian-Sudanese relations, already symbolized by the con-

ciliatory actions of Mahu Bey Urfali, who had governed at Berber
and then temporarily at Khartoum after the death of Uthman Bey
in 1825. Mahu Bey set out to regain the confidence of the Sudanese:
he reduced taxes and sought Sudanese participation in government
by appointing the respected Sudanese notable Abd al-Qadir wad al-
Zayn as his official adviser. Ali Khurshid not only confirmed these
policies when he arrived in Khartoum in 1826, but expanded the
reforms of Mahu Bey, always in close consultation with Abd al-Qadir.
The many peasants who had fled into the hinterland were encouraged to return to their lands along the river and in the Gezira.
Letters of amnesty were granted to fugitives, and promises were made
to respect the property and persons of the Sudanese. An equitable
system of taxation was drawn up in consultation with Sudanese
notables, and the very powerful and influential class of holy men and
shaykhs were won over to the administration by tax exemptions.
But Ali Khurshid was not content merely to restore the Sudan to
its previous condition. Under his initiative trade routes were protected and expanded, Khartoum was developed, and a host of agricultural and technical improvements were undertaken. In all these
accomplishments and projects Sudanese notables were consulted and
taken into the confidence of the administration, so that the Sudanese
were not entirely ignored by a regime outwardly characterized by
autocratic absolutism. When Ali Khurshid retired to Cairo in 1838,
he left behind a prosperous and contented country, a more fitting
tribute to his administrative abilities than the many honors bestowed
upon him by Muhammad Ali.

Ahmad Pasha abu Adhan succeeded Ali Khurshid and with but
few exceptions continued his policies. As before, the Sudanese were
consulted, and Abd al-Qadir remained the official adviser to the
government. As before, the development of Khartoum continued,
and trade, industry, and agriculture expanded. But unlike the more
casual Khurshid, Abu Adhan made it his primary concern to root
out corruption and peculation, and he dealt ruthlessly with such
offenders or those who sought to thwart his schemes to reorganize
taxation. He was particularly fond of the army, which reaped the
benefits of regular pay and tolerable conditions in return for the
brunt of the expansion and consolidation of Egyptian administration
in Kasala and among the Baqqara of southern Kordofan. Efficient
administration, however, appeared to Muhammad Ali as an attempt
at independence if not disloyalty on the part of his subordinate in

Khartoum, suspicions which were not dispelled by the rumors and intrigues which circulated at Muhammad Ali's court in Cairo. Abu Adhan was thus recalled to Cairo in the autumn of 1843, but he mysteriously died of poison before he left the Sudan. His financial officials were perhaps relieved at his death, and the taxpayers probably not unhappy to be rid of his just but violent efficiency, but neither realized that the days of peace and prosperity in the Sudan were rapidly drawing to a close.

After the death of Abu Adhan the Sudan slipped into twenty years of stagnation and decay caused principally by the absence of strong governors-general at Khartoum and vacillation by the viceroys at Cairo. The success of any authoritarian regime such as the Egyptian administration in the Sudan depends primarily on the vigor and the abilities of the ruler and the opportunity to carry out his policies. Unhappily for the Sudan, if the successors of Abu Adhan possessed administrative talent, they were seldom able to demonstrate it. Alarmed by the independent attitude of Abu Adhan, Muhammad Ali first decentralized the administration by abolishing the office of governor-general and requiring governors of each Sudanese province to report directly to Cairo. Then, just as suddenly, he revived the office of governor-general but sought to control its incumbents by limiting their tenure to a few short years at most, to a few long months at least. Thus no governor-general held office long enough to introduce his own plans, let alone carry on those of his predecessor. New schemes were never begun, old projects were allowed to languish, and the administration of the Sudan slid into neglect and abandonment. Without direction the army and the bureaucracy became demoralized and indifferent, while the Sudanese became disgruntled with a government that gave little service in return for taxes and increasingly dissatisfied with a regime which ignored Sudanese advice, particularly after the death in 1857 of Abd al-Qadir. The vacillation at Cairo and the apathy at Khartoum cannot be attributed alone to the dotage of Muhammad Ali. His second successor as viceroy of Egypt, Said, was so dismayed by what he saw in the Sudan during his tour of 1857 that he considered abandoning the country altogether. He might as well have done so, for he revived Muhammad Ali's schemes of decentralization and divided the Sudan into four districts, each in direct communication with Cairo. Said hoped that such a system of decentralized administration would strengthen the Sudan. In reality it only managed to perpetuate the inertia of the bureaucracy, the demoralization of the army, and the stagnation of Sudanese economic and cultural life until the more dynamic Ismail took over the guidance of Egyptian and Sudanese affairs in 1862.

During these quiescent decades, however, two ominous developments began which presaged future problems. Reacting to pressure from the Western powers, particularly Great Britain, the governor-general of the Sudan was ordered in December 1854 to halt the slave trade, and in the following year a control station was established at Fashoda. Although Said sincerely hoped to suppress the trade, not even the viceroy himself could overcome established custom with the stroke of a pen and the erection of a few police posts. Clearly, none of the antislave-trade crusaders, English or Egyptian, ever imagined the disasters which were to follow this great humanitarian step. But if the restriction of the slave trade precipitated resistance among the Sudanese, the appointment of Christian officials to the administration and the expansion of the European Christian community caused open resentment. The appointment of Arakil Bey al-Armani, an Armenian Christian, as governor at Khartoum in 1857 shocked the Sudanese, particularly the Shukriyya, but the hostility generated by this appointment never had time to erupt into open rebellion because of the governor's death the following year. Nevertheless, the precedent of appointing Christian administrators had been established, with fateful consequences for subsequent administrations. During these same years the European community at Khartoum gradually increased, spurred by the abolition of state monopolies on many articles of trade. Mostly of Mediterranean origins, the European merchants were either ignored or tolerated by the Sudanese and confined their contacts to compatriots within their own community and to the Turkish officials whose manners and dress they frequently adopted. They became a powerful and influential group, whose lasting contribution to the Sudan was their lead taken in opening the Southern Sudan to navigation and commerce, thereby bringing the vast Negroid, equatorial regions of the upper Nile into the orbit of Sudanese history.

In 1863 Ismail Pasha became viceroy of Egypt. Educated in Egypt, Vienna, and Paris, Ismail had absorbed the European interest in overseas adventures as well as Muhammad Ali's desire for imperial expansion. The Sudan was not excluded from his imaginative and expansive schemes for transforming Egypt into a modern state by employing Western technology. First he hoped to acquire the rest of the Nile basin, including the Southern Sudan and the inter-lacustrine Bantu states by the Great Lakes of Central Africa. To finance such a vast undertaking, not to mention the projects for the modernization of Egypt itself, Ismail turned to those capital surplus nations of Europe whose people were willing to risk their savings at high rates of interest in the cause of Egyptian and African development. But such funds would clearly be attracted only as long as Ismail demonstrated his interest in reform by intensifying the campaign against the slave trade in the Sudan. Ismail needed no encouragement. Like Said, he was genuinely opposed to the slave trade and made sincere efforts to suppress it and to cooperate with the European powers toward that end. Thus these two major themes of Ismail's rule of the Sudan—imperial expansion and the suppression of the slave trade—became inextricably intertwined, culminating in a third major development, the introduction of the ever-increasing number of European Christians to carry out the herculean task of modernization. In the Sudan all three of these explosive themes were soon united in the splendid figure of Samuel White Baker.

In 1869 Ismail commissioned Baker to lead an expedition up the White Nile to establish Egyptian hegemony over the equatorial regions of Central Africa and to curtail the slave trade on the upper Nile. Baker was a Christian and an Englishman in a devoutly Muslim land. Although the expedition was unable to make its way through the Nile swamps until April 1871, Baker, once he had reached Gondokoro, relentlessly imposed Egyptian authority over the slavers. He appropriated their trading stations and established an Egyptian government monopoly over the ivory trade, so that the Khartoum merchants either withdrew or joined the Egyptian service, hoping for better and more profitable days in the future.

Baker had less success asserting Egyptian rule over the indigenous inhabitants. On the one hand, he earned the implacable hostility of the Bari by raiding for supplies he could not acquire by any other means, but, on the other, he won the support of the Acholi by curbing the activities of the powerful slaving firm of Muhammad Ahmad al-Aqqad and his successor Muhammad Abu Suud. In April 1872 Baker crossed the Victoria Nile into Bunyoro, hoping to annex that kingdom to Egypt's growing empire in equatorial Africa. He failed. The ruler of Bunyoro, Kabarega, had no use for the protection of the khedive of Egypt and forced Baker back across the Victoria Nile to his stations in the Equatoria Province.

Baker returned to Europe and fame and fortune. Behind in the Sudan he had extended Egyptian power and curbed the slave traders on the Nile, but he had also alienated certain African tribes like the Bari and, being a rather tactless Christian, Ismail's Muslim administrators as well. Moreover, Baker had really struck only at the Nilotic slave trade. Beyond to the west, on the vast plains of the Bahr al-Ghazal, slave merchants had established enormous empires with a complex of stations (*zariba*), recruited large private slave armies (the soldiers of which were known as *bazinqir*), and made offensive alliances with neighboring tribes. From these stations scattered over the Bahr al-Ghazal the long lines of human chattels were sent overland through Darfur and Kordofan to the slave markets of the Northern Sudan, Egypt, and Arabia. Not only did the firearms of the Khartoumers (as the traders were called) establish their supremacy over the African tribes, but those merchants with the strongest resources gradually swallowed up lesser traders until virtually the whole of the Bahr al-Ghazal was controlled by the greatest slaver of them all, al-Zubayr Rahma Mansur, more commonly known as Zobeir Pasha. So powerful had he become that in 1873, the year Baker retired from the Sudan, the khedive appointed al-Zubayr governor of the Bahr al-Ghazal. Ismail's officials had failed to destroy al-Zubayr as Baker had crushed the firm of al-Aqqad on the Victoria Nile, and to elevate al-Zubayr to the governorship was the only way to establish at least the nominal sovereignty of Cairo over that enormous province. Thus the agents of al-Zubayr continued to pillage the Bahr al-Ghazal under the Egyptian flag, while officially Egypt extended its dominion to the tropical rainforests of the Congo.

Despite his shortcomings, Baker had succeeded in Equatoria while the khedive's Muslim officials had failed in the Bahr al-Ghazal. To replace Baker, therefore, Ismail sought another European, and he offered the governorship of the Equatoria Province to Charles George Gordon, who in China had won fame and the sobriquet "Chinese" Gordon. Gordon arrived in Equatoria in 1874. His object was the same as Baker's—to consolidate Egyptian authority in Equatoria and to establish Egyptian sovereignty over the interlacustrine kingdoms of the Great Lakes—but his means were considerably more pacific. He reasserted government control over the stations which had, since the departure of Baker, been used once again as slave centers by the traders, and stopped the continual foraging raids against the riverine tribes. But Gordon's goal was the lakes, not the river, and he sought to bring Bunyoro and Buganda to recognize Egyptian sovereignty. Like Baker, he failed. Although he established stations beyond the Victoria Nile in Bunyoro proper at Foweira and Mruli, his resources were never sufficient to accomplish by force what he could not achieve by peaceful negotiation. When Gordon retired from Equatoria in 1877, the interlacustrine kingdoms remained stubbornly independent.

But if Gordon failed to expand the khedive's empire toward the equator, Ismail's other agents were having greater success in Darfur in the west and at Suakin and Massawa in the east. Despite the defeat of the Fur army at Bara in 1821, Darfur had always remained beyond the sphere of Egyptian control. To al-Zubayr, the slave-trading governor of the Bahr al-Ghazal, Darfur represented an untapped source of slaves and loot, and so he marched northward from the Bahr al-Ghazal and defeated the Fur army at Al Manawashi in October 1874. The Egyptian government at once sought to capitalize on al-Zubayr's conquest and rushed an expeditionary force of Egyptian troops under Ismail Ayyub Pasha westward from Kordofan. Finding his authority challenged by the administration at Khartoum, al-Zubayr journeyed to Egypt to present his case before Ismail and to win khedivial recognition for his position in Darfur. This blunder was his undoing. The khedive placed al-Zubayr under house arrest in Cairo, and without his leadership his far-flung slave-trading empire eventually collapsed before Egyptian forces led by the Italian, Romolo Gessi. In 1879 Gessi defeated al-Zubayr's son and successor, Sulayman, and effectively established Egyptian authority in the Bahr al-Ghazal. Meanwhile in Darfur another Italian, G. B. Messedaglia, and later the famous Austrian adventurer, Rudolf von Slatin, consolidated Egyptian control in Darfur.

Ismail's eastward expansion was never as successful as his operations in the south and west. In 1865 the ports of Suakin and Massawa were ceded to Ismail, and in 1871 a Swiss, Munzinger, was made governor of Massawa to prepare for Egyptian extension into Ethiopia. An Egyptian expeditionary force followed in 1875-76 but was overwhelmed by the Ethiopians and driven back to its fortified position on the Red Sea coast. The dismal ending of the Ethiopian affair marks the close of Ismail's efforts at expansion, for although the khedive no doubt continued to dream of remote African conquests, his resources were rapidly dwindling and his foreign creditors were increasingly reluctant to finance Egyptian modernization, let alone expansion. But just as Egyptian rule in the Sudan was weakened by its extension into the new provinces, devouring men, money, and materials in alarming proportions, its effectiveness in controlling the heartland of the Sudan was compromised by drastic economies at precisely the time when the two latently explosive policies of Ismail's Sudanese policy—the campaign against the slave trade and the appointment of European, Christian officials—were ignited by the appointment of Gordon as governor-general of the Sudan in 1877.

Gordon was the first European, Christian governor-general of the Sudan. He returned to the Sudan with the intent of leading the crusade against the slave trade, and to assist him in this great humanitarian enterprise, he surrounded himself with a cadre of European and American Christian officials. In 1877 Ismail had signed the Anglo-Egyptian Slave Trade Convention, which provided for the termination of the sale and purchase of slaves in the Sudan by 1880. Gordon set out to fulfill the terms of this treaty and in whirlwind tours through the country broke up the markets and imprisoned the traders. His European subordinates did the same in the provinces. Indeed, the moral fervor of Victorian society complimented Gordon's own unorthodox but Calvinist-oriented religious views and his sympathy for the underdog. The combination created the perfect crusader of him, just as it blinded him to his invidious position as a Christian in a Muslim land and obscured from him the social and economic effects of arbitrary repression. Not only did Gordon's anti-slave-trade crusade create a crisis in the Sudan's economy, but the Sudanese soon came to believe that the crusade, led by European Christians, violated the principles and traditions of Islam. By 1879 a strong current of reaction against Gordon's reforms was running through the Sudan. The powerful slave-trading interests had, of course, turned against the administration, while the ordinary villagers and nomads, who habitually blamed the government for any difficulties, were quick to associate economic depression with the religious transgressions of the Christian governor-general. And then suddenly, in the midst of rising discontent in the Sudan, Ismail's financial position collapsed. In difficulties for years, he could now no longer pay the interest on the Egyptian debt, and an international commission was appointed by the European powers to oversee Egyptian finances. After sixteen years of glorious spending, Ismail sailed away into exile. Gordon resigned.

Behind in the Sudan Gordon left a perilous situation. The Sudanese were confused and dissatisfied. Many of the ablest senior officials, both European and Egyptian, had been dismissed by Gordon, departed with him, or died in his service. The bureaucracy, which after all made the administration function, had been castigated and ignored by Gordon, and its officials had lapsed into apathy and dismay, wanting only to return to Egypt. Moreover, the office of governor-general, on which the administration was so dependent, devolved upon Muhammad Rauf Pasha, a mild man, ill-suited to stem the current of discontent or to shore up the structure of Egyptian rule, particularly when he could no longer count on Egyptian resources. Such then was the Sudan in June of 1881 when Muhammad Ahmad declared himself to be the Mahdi.

Muhammad Ahmad ibn Abd Allah was the son of a Dunqulawi boatbuilder who claimed descent from the Prophet. Deeply religious from his youth, he was educated in one of the Sufi orders, the Sammaniya, but he became disgusted with the worldly ways of his teacher and secluded himself on Aba Island in the White Nile to practice religious asceticism. In 1880 he toured Kordofan, where he learned of the discontent of the people and observed those actions of the government which he could not reconcile with his own religious beliefs. Upon his return to Aba Island he clearly viewed himself as a *mujaddid*, a renewer of the Muslim faith, and his mission, to reform Islam and return it to the pristine form practiced by the Prophet. To Muhammad Ahmad the orthodox *ulama* who supported the administration were no less infidels than Christians, and when he later lashed out against misgovernment, he was referring as much to the theological heresy as to secular maladministration. Once he had assumed the Mahdiship, Muhammad Ahmad was not regarded by the Sudanese simply as a reformer but also as an eschatological figure, one who foreshadows the end of an age of darkness (which happened to coincide with the end of the thirteenth Muslim century) and heralds the beginnings of a new era of light and righteousness. Thus, as a divinely guided reformer and symbol, Muhammad Ahmad fulfilled the requirements of Mahdiship in the eyes of his supporters.

Surrounding the Mahdi were his followers, the Ansar, and foremost among them was Abd Allahi ibn Muhammad, the Khalifa, who came from the Taaisha tribe of the Baqqara Arabs and who assumed the leadership of the Mahdist state upon the death of Muhammad Ahmad. The holy men, the *fakis*, who for long had lamented the sorry state of religion in the Sudan brought on by the legalistic and unappealing orthodoxy of the Egyptians, looked to the Mahdi to purge the Sudan of the faithless ones. Also in his following, more numerous and powerful than the holy men, were the merchants formerly connected with the slave trade. All had suffered from Gordon's campaign against the trade, and all now hoped to reassert their economic position under the banner of religious war. Neither of these groups, however, could have carried out a revolution by themselves. The third and vital participants were the Baqqara Arabs, the cattle nomads of Kordofan and Darfur who hated taxes and despised government. They formed the shock troops of the Mahdist revolutionary army, whose enthusiasm and numbers more than made up for its primitive technology.

By its fumbling attempts to arrest the Mahdi and proscribe his movement, the government only managed to enhance his prestige and convince the Sudanese that after all perhaps Muhammad Ahmad was truly *the* Mahdi. Two expeditions launched against him in 1881 were surprised and annihilated by the Ansar, and a third sent in May 1882 was similarly wiped out. By September 1882 the Mahdists controlled all of Kordofan and were beseiging the provincial capital of El Obeid; in January 1883 the town capitulated after a heroic defense. The Mahdist forces rapidly increased as a result of their continuous victories. Although the first ineffectual attempts to crush the revolt can be ascribed to the incapacity of the governor-general, Muhammad Rauf, the pessimism and paralysis which overcame the administration in the Sudan can only be explained by the events in Egypt which culminated in the British occupation of 1882.

Having taken on Egypt, the British were disinclined to extend their obligations to the Sudan. They had no real interests in the Sudan, and they felt that Egyptian finances would only be further drained and disrupted by large military expenditures to combat the Mahdists. Nevertheless, the khedive and his ministers desperately required a victory of any sort to add luster to a prestige tarnished by their dependence on British power. With considerable misgivings the British authorities allowed the Egyptian government to organize one final military expedition to crush the Mahdi. The expedition was commanded by Colonel William Hicks of the Indian army.

Under his direction ten thousand troops were assembled at Khartoum in the autumn of 1883 and marched into Kordofan to find the Mahdi. Although it appeared formidable, the expedition was in fact doomed from the start. Hicks and his Egyptian officers quarreled. The troops, many of whom had arrived in Khartoum from Egypt in chains, were demoralized, and on the march the expedition was harassed by Sudanese guerrillas and deluged with propaganda predicting the certain defeat of the infidels before the soldiers of God. On November 5, 1883, at Shaykan, south of El Obeid, Hicks and his ten thousand were annihilated. He and his troops died fighting to the last, but it was a futile gesture against men who, perhaps after all, were the soldiers of God.

After Shaykan the Sudan was lost. The provinces of Darfur and the Bahr al-Ghazal surrendered to the Mahdists, and the revolt swept into the Gezira and beyond to the Beja of the Red Sea Hills until only the Red Sea ports in the east, Equatoria in the south, and the Nile north of Dunqula remained in Egyptian hands. There was now no question of saving the Sudan; the only problem was finding someone who could evacuate the hapless Egyptian garrisons. In the words of Sir Rivers Wilson, "If you want some out-of-the-way piece of work to be done in an unknown and barbarous country, Gordon would be your man." [5] Most everyone agreed, and so Gordon went out to the Sudan for a third time on a mission still charged with controversy and obscured by misunderstanding. The British government in London officially sent Gordon to report on the best means to affect a withdrawal of the Egyptian garrisons. The British officials in Egypt thought Gordon was to carry out an evacuation. As for Gordon himself, his ideas were at best contradictory, at worst confused, but by the time he reached Khartoum in February 1884, he contemplated neither negotiation with the Mahdi nor peaceful evacuation. The only alternative was to await a relief column strong enough to lead the Egyptian garrison to safety. Thus Gordon arranged the defense of Khartoum and waited. In October the Mahdi himself appeared to establish his headquarters across the White Nile at Omdurman. Meanwhile a relief expedition was organized and in a leisurely manner made its way up the Nile. Increasingly apprehensive over the imminent appearance of British troops, the Mahdi determined to storm the city. Weakened by the long siege, the garrison

[5] Sir C. Rivers Wilson, *Chapters From My Official Life* (London: 1916), p. 200.

could not check the Mahdist assault on January 26, 1885. The Ansar easily broke through the Khartoum defenses, swarmed into the city, and massacred the defenders, including Gordon. Two days later the steamers of the relief column arrived to find Khartoum deserted and in ruins. The Turkiya was over.

Although Egyptian administration in the Sudan had disappeared, sixty years of Turko-Egyptian rule left a lasting impact on the country. For the first time the peoples inhabiting the great basin of the Nile from Lake Albert to the Egyptian frontier had been brought under a single government. True, that government was corrupt and mismanaged, but such characteristics were not new to the Sudan. The Muslims of the Northern Sudan experienced the rule of a new and wider sphere of authority represented by the centralized, autocratic institutions of Egyptian administration. Conditioned in the past to respect the local authoritarianism of the village and the tribe and the religious autocracy of the holy men, the Northern Sudanese had to accommodate themselves during the Turkiya to the impersonal power of the state. Such authority may not have been always effective, but the recognition of centralized authority during the Turkiya helped to prepare the Northern Sudanese for the autocracy of the Khalifa and the absolutism of British imperial administration.

The Turkiya also extended Egyptian control up the Nile into the Southern Sudan. Although Ismail considered the equatorial regions as outlying provinces of his empire, they were attached to the Sudan by the slave trade and the Egyptian administration in the Sudan. The dismal effects of the slave trade and the bitter feelings which have lingered long after its suppression have done little to assuage the enmity of the Southern Sudanese toward the Northerners. The introduction of Egyptian administration certainly opened the Southern Sudan to the outside world, but its maladministration never provided any beneficent services for the Southern Sudanese in return for the burdens heaped upon them. Today the sullen hostility between the Northern and Southern Sudanese threatens the very unity of the Sudan. The beginnings of that hostility are to be found in the Turkiya.

If Egyptian administration in the Sudan was corrupt, at least it introduced the Sudanese to the new technology imported from Europe to Egypt and passed on into the Sudan by the technicians sent to modernize and thereby to strengthen the administration's hold on the outlying provinces of the Egyptian empire. Telegraph, postal service, and steamers provided more rapid communication that did much to tie the various regions of the Sudan together and to convince many Sudanese of the power and usefulness of European technology. Indeed, the Khalifa sought to utilize this new technology in the service of the Mahdist state and became extremely dependent on the few Egyptian technicians remaining after the fall of Khartoum. Their presence during the Mahdiya provided continuity in the use of modern technology which the British were to develop and refine in the twentieth century.

Although the Mahdists destroyed much of Egyptian culture and orthodox Islam in the Sudan, the influence of both had become so pervasive during the sixty years of the Turkiya that they quickly blossomed again under the protection of the British imperium. During the Turkiya Arabic books, periodicals, and newspapers from Egypt were read in the Sudan, and the schools were staffed by teachers from Egypt employing texts and curricula fashioned in Egyptian schools. The strong religious ties between Egypt and the Sudan in the twentieth century arise from the earlier, more tenuous relations of the Turkiya. Although obscured by the Mahdist upheaval and subordinated by the power of the British administration in the Sudan, the legacy of the Egyptian presence during the nineteenth century remains one of the vital influences shaping the modern Sudan.

FOUR

BRITAIN AND THE NILE VALLEY

Britain in Egypt, 1875-1952

Even though the British did not occupy it until 1882, Egypt had begun to slip under European political controls as early as 1875. Before the British invasion the Khedive Ismail had been deposed and a nationalist movement, the Arabi revolt, had occurred. Financial insolvency was, of course, Ismail's greatest stumbling–block. He was compelled by Egypt's staggering debt to create the *Caisse de la Dette Publique,* an international financial body, representing the interests in Egypt of English, French, Austrian, Russian, German, and Italian bondholders. He was also forced to appoint British and French advisers over the ministries of finance and public works. But Khedive Ismail was too ambitious a man to concede this weakening of his authority. Here his interests coincided with those of other social groups and with the growth of nationalist sentiments. The result was the beginning of the Arabi revolt in 1879.

Early Egyptian nationalism—if indeed the Arabi revolt can be called that—had many sources. Clearly, one of the most important was Islam. Islam was a major area of consensus and appeal in Egypt. Thus, it was not uncommon for these early nationalists to sound the warning that Islam was in danger. Some important alterations had in fact taken place within Islam as a result of its contacts with the West and with modernization. Western scholarship was extremely critical of Islam, regarding it as a regressive force in society or, if not regressive, at least an obstacle to further progress. Furthermore, the contacts that Egyptians had with European civilization, such as Tahtawi's experiences in France, opened the eyes of the educated to the achievements of Europe. The progressive school in Islam sought to bring their religion more in line with their understanding of the West. They emphasized the rationality of Islam and argued that Islam was completely compatible with modern science. They also stressed its egalitarianism and the sophistication and elevation of its moral system.

These Islamic reformers were deeply involved in political questions as well as religious and intellectual matters. They were intensely concerned about political weakness in the whole Islamic East in the face of European encroachments into the region. They became champions of a reformed Islam, powerful enough to withstand pressure from the West. Some of the most brilliant members of this group were Egyptians who lived in Egypt during the 1860s and 1870s. They wrote for and edited newspapers. They attempted to organize societies for the propagation of their ideas, and in their publications they spoke of the need for Muslims to work together, to reform their institutions, to adopt modern technology, and to frustrate the aggressive goals of the Europeans in the Islamic world.

Without a doubt the most energetic, if not the most influential, of these Islamic leaders was Jamal al-Din al-Afghani, who spent the 1870's in Egypt. A well traveled writer, and above all else a political agitator, Afghani wished to rally pan-Islamic sentiment as a unifying force among Muslim countries against the enrcoachments of the West. There is some question about his devoutness in personal belief. Certainly his religious views, if they were sincerely held, were far from orthodox and were deeply colored by political concerns.[1] While at al-Azhar he was able to influence a younger generation with his political ideas, but because of his agitation, the khedive eventually decided to exile him, for he constituted as great a threat to established Egyptian authority as to the interests of the Europeans.

Islamic nationalism in Egypt was thus one of the major intellectual bases of the Arabi revolt. A second was a more westernized form of nationalism, deriving its inspiration from liberal European nationalism. The westernized nationalists wanted Egypt to be transformed into a territorial, secular nation-state and felt that a person's allegiance in political matters should be to state rather than religion. These men sought the unity of Copt and Muslim alike in allegiance to the state. They, too, were conscious of Western strength, fearful of Western designs upon Egypt. Their formula, however, was not to invoke Islam, but rather to achieve a secular national ideal.

It is much too easy to assume that intellectuals provided the

[1] Sylvia Haim, *Arab Nationalism* (Berkeley, Calif.: 1962).

spark for the Arabi revolt. We have their writings, exhorting the people to unite and resist Western control, but these men probably had less actual influence than historical judgment has accorded them. The literarcy rate in Egypt was not high. The newspapers in which they wrote did not have wide circulations. Moreover, Jamal al-Din al-Afghani was not a prolific writer, and his influence was largely confined to a circle of students and protégés. The cutting edge of the revolt came, instead, from other groups in Egypt, groups with less sophisticated nationalist or pan-Islamic ideas but with a definite set of grievances and a desire to alter the *status quo*. Three are deserving of attention: the army, the civil service, and the peasantry.

The revolt was ignited in the army. By the late 1870s the military was torn by strife and discontent. The frustrating campaigns in Ethiopia had taken their toll on morale, much as the Palestinian war of 1948 was to influence the army seventy years later. Military leaders, especially the junior officers, were convinced that their defeats were caused by the inefficiency of the government. The financial plight of Egypt had hit the army hard; salaries were in arrears, and the size of the army was being reduced. By far the greatest source of tension within the army was between junior Egyptian officers and the senior Turkish officer corps. In some important ways the army was still an instrument of foreign control and domination as it had been under the Mamluks and even under Muhammad Ali. The highest positions in the army, as well as the civil bureaucracy and the landed aristocracy, were still held by alien Turks and Circassians. Native-born Egyptian Arabs had begun to move into the officer ranks, but as yet the highest rank they held was that of colonel. Moreover, as reductions in the size of the army were made, Egyptian officers were dropped much more frequently than Turks or Circassians. The disaffected military elements began to organize under the leadership of three colonels—Ahmad Arabi, Ali Fahmi, and Sami al-Barudi. They founded a secret society within the army, unified by their discontent with religious laxity, economic depression, and social discrimination.

Learning of the existence of this group, Ismail saw an opportunity to use it for his own ends. With the khedive's encouragement the army officers were emboldened to create a formal National Party. Then they interjected themselves into Egypt's troubled relationship with the European powers. In 1879 they drafted a "Manifesto of the Egyptian National Party," repudiating foreign influence in the administration of Egypt, guaranteeing the payment of foreign debts if no Egyptian property was pawned, and calling for the return to Egypt of khedivial domains and railroad revenues.[2] Ismail tried to use the upsurge of nationalist sentiments to rid his regime of foreign controls, and he promptly dismissed the British and French advisers from the government. Ismail's plans were too radical, however. They encountered European opposition, and under this pressure Ismail was deposed in 1879 in favor of his son Tawfiq. The British and French advisers were reinstalled. On the surface, pre-1879 conditions had been restored, but the discontented element within the army remained, biding its time for further opportunities to challenge the ruling order.

Similar problems beset the Egyptian government bureaucracy. There were arrears in salary and a growing discontent with European control over the administration. As usual, the peasantry bore the full brunt of the economic crisis. Taxes were extraordinarily high, for they had been increased continually throughout the nineteenth century. Upon occasion the government even attempted to collect them twice a year. In 1878-79 a poor harvest brought famine. The peasantry were not much influenced by nationalist aspirations, but their traditional resentment against the oppression and exploitation of the government was heightened by these harsh economic conditions. They were anxious to throw off the yoke of the government in the hope of ridding themselves of their heavy taxes.

All these tensions culminated in the rebellions of 1881-82, known generally as the Arabi revolt because of the central role played by the army and Ahmad Arabi. The rebel army leaders became gradually more radical, especially as they encountered opposition to their original goals. Their first demands were rather specific and not notably anti-European: removal of military grievances, the end of Turkish and Circassian privileges, the implementation of a constitution, and the creation of a regular parliament. But soon radical elements came to the fore and began to threaten European interests. In particular, the radicals demanded the right to debate the Egyptian budget within the Egyptian parliament (Council of Notables). The European powers were reluctant to grant this demand because of its threat to the allocation of debt payments. This created an impasse

[2] The Manifesto was published only after the deposition of Ismail but indicates the currents of thought among Egyptians at the time.

among the rebels, the khedive and his conservative supporters, and the European powers. Rioting broke out in Lower Egypt, and a number of Christians were killed. To restore order, preserve the European bondholders, and above all secure the Suez Canal, the British finally decided in 1882 to intervene. Once the radical military element had taken control of the movement, the Arabi revolt was doomed to failure, not simply because of probable European intervention but because of inadequate leadership. Early in the rebellion army leaders had worked in alliance with liberal and progressive Egyptian ministers. But the alliance had been broken; much of the civilian element had withdrawn in protest against the drift to more radical and anti-European measures. By late 1881 Ahmad Arabi and his officers were in full charge of the rebellion. They had taken over the Egyptian government; Tawfiq was in opposition to them, but powerless to resist. The revolutionary leaders were not, however, adequately prepared for their responsibilities. Arabi himself had only a military education, although he was definitely influenced by pan-Islamic aspirations through a short association with al-Azhar during his military career. He knew no European language, and his knowledge of European civilization was derived from having read a few European works available in Arabic translation. The whole Arabi ministry had only one member fluent in a European language. In general, its members had an inadequate appreciation of the power of Europe and of the programs needed to modernize Egypt. Nor was the army an efficient military organization, and it was certainly no match for the British troops which invaded the country from the Suez Canal, routed the Egyptian army at Tel el Kebir, and occupied Cairo. Khedive Tawfiq was returned from his temporary exile at Alexandria, accompanied by British troops, and the leaders of the rebellion were exiled to Ceylon. The British occupation of Egypt had begun.

The cardinal fact of British rule in Egypt was that Britain's responsibilities for governing Egypt were never total and her powers were inadequately defined. The British were reluctant invaders, hesitant to assume the full powers of government. Hence their impact on Egypt was limited, their programs of social change circumscribed.

In 1882 the pace of European imperial expansion was quickening. The Liberal Party of Gladstone was in power in Britain, and his opposition to the extension of the British Empire was well known. Nevertheless, the Gladstonian ministry itself called for the dispatch of troops to Egypt. The British tried unsuccessfully to find solutions other than armed force. They turned to the Turks, and they considered a combined occupation with the French. But the great stumbling block was always the Suez Canal. By the 1880s it had become the lifeline to empire and trade in the East. The British government could not afford to have any other major power astride this waterway, and thus, in an effort to safeguard the security of the Canal and to insure that it was not dominated by any other power, the British occupied Egypt. At the same time, in order to allay European criticism and the attacks of antiimperialist critics in England, the Liberal ministry promised rapid evacuation once order had been restored in Egypt. This promise, repeated upon numerous occasions, made the British position in Egypt anomalous. Since a hasty evacuation had been indicated, although it was not forthcoming, the British could not assume full control over internal Egyptian affairs. The capitulatory privileges enjoyed by foreign communities remained. The international financial bodies created by Ismail, such as the *Caisse de la Dette Publique*, also continued to function. Moreover, the French were deeply opposed to British power in Egypt because of their own close ties and interests there, and the French government used its rather considerable power in Egypt to make Britain's task of governing even more difficult. Laboring under these limitations, the British were inclined to keep Egyptian institutions intact. British officials governed behind and through Egyptian ministers, but some measure of independent Egyptian power remained and was a source of repeated conflicts between the British and ruling Egyptian elements.

Ever since the publication of Hobson's famous *Imperialism, A Study* (1902), Egypt has been used as an example to prove the economic interpretation of imperialism. According to Hobson and men of like mind, Egypt was occupied by the British in order to protect the interests of European bondholders. The European financial community was felt to be the moving force in bringing about the British invasion. There is a great deal in this theory. The Egyptian debt was £100 million by 1880, held mainly by influential British and French banking houses. Economic disorganization in Egypt, producing high taxes and arrears in salary payments to civil servants and military officers, created the conditions for revolt. Moreover, in the crucial years of 1881-82 there was the struggle over who should control the Egyptian budget. But these pressures in themselves might not have led to a British invasion. In fact, the radical section of the Liberal Party opposed invasion for just these reasons. They did not want to be associated with an operation which appeared only to be in the interests of European capitalists, and the British government had earlier even advised that the debts be repudiated. The crucial factor, tipping the balance in favor of occupation, was the Suez Canal.

The two factors of limited British powers in Egypt and the strategic importance of the Suez Canal to British imperial interests shaped Britain's techniques of rule and its impact on Egyptian development. These two factors tended to make British rule conservative. The overriding goal of the British was to secure the tranquility of Egypt and the prevention of internal disorders. This concern for stability was heightened in turn by the fact that Britain's position in Egypt was so ill-defined. Another Arabi revolt could lead to international disputes, especially between England and France, and even to concerted European efforts to push Britain out of Egypt. Egyptian stability was to be attained in part by limited and controlled modernization. The fond hope of British administrators in Egypt was to create rising standards of living and win some measure of support for their regime through modernizing reforms. But stability was also to be attained by preserving important aspects of the *status quo.* British officials were reluctant, for example, to effect far-reaching changes in the Egyptian social structure for fear of disruptive consequences. Also, they were hesitant to tamper with the basic administrative system of the country. It is for this reason that on the whole the British tended to extend patterns of nineteenth-century development rather than to introduce new ones. In particular, the old social divisions of ruling landed aristocratics, a rising but not fully accepted salaried middle class, and an oppressed peasantry were retained through the period of British influence. It was in the period from 1882 to 1918 that the British had their strongest impact on Egypt. After World War I the British began to disengage themselves from internal Egyptian administration, limiting their role to safeguarding crucial imperial interests in Egypt.

The architect of early British administration in Egypt was Lord Cromer (Evelyn Baring), British consul-general in Egypt from 1883 to 1907. Before his appointment as consul-general he had been one of the commissioners of Egypt's public debt and from 1880 to 1883 financial adviser to the British viceroy of India. He had demonstrated extraordinary administrative and financial abilities in India, and his task in Egypt in these early years was clear: to reorganize Egyptian finances and restore the country to solvency. He was an autocrat, known in India as the "vice-viceroy" and called "Over-Baring" by subordinates in Egypt. But he was able to attract good men to work in Egypt and soon surrounded himself with a small but efficient group of senior British officials. Through tireless administrative vigilance these officials were able to set Egyptian finances in order by the late 1880s and then in the succeeding two decades to bring prosperity to the country. On the other hand, his autocratic methods eventually alienated some of his own British personnel and especially educated Egyptians. But though he was not loved by the Egyptian intelligentsia, he was respected, even feared, because of his rigorous honesty and dedication to duty.

Cromer was raised a Benthamite and liberal, and had even thought of running for Parliament as a liberal. He carried over his Benthamite reforming tendencies into his colonial experiences. But his liberalism and Benthamism were tempered by Egyptian exigencies, and he carried forward programs of social change in keeping with Britain's imperial goals. Consequently, the areas in which the British had the greatest impact were finance, hydraulics, agriculture, trade and communications. Those least affected were education, parliamentary institutions, and industrial development.

Cromer hoped to achieve stability by increasing agricultural productivity through irrigation improvements and by reducing taxation. The three decades before the outbreak of World War I were unparalleled for hydraulic achievement, at least until the present day. British engineers, most of them brought to Egypt from India, first restored the barrage across the Nile near Cairo. This had been constructed during the reigns of Muhammad Ali and Ismail, but the work had been done so imperfectly that the barrage could never really be used. By 1890 the barrage was put in working order and was able to perform its functions of raising the Nile water level and providing irrigation water for the Egyptian delta. British engineers also corrected defects in the irrigation system, realigning canals, using dredges to remove silt from canals, and digging new canals. It was during these years that the *corvée* (labor tax used to dig and clean canals) was abolished. The British were revolted by the inhumanity of this practice and were also convinced that machinery could do a more efficient job than unpaid labor. The most spectacular event of these years was the construction of a large dam at Aswan, completed in 1902.

All of these impressive hydraulic works permitted an extension of perennial irrigation and an increase in the amount of arable land and the number of crops the soil could support each year. Cotton cultivation grew by leaps and bounds, crowding all other export commodities out of the trading statistics. It was in this period that Egypt first became an importer of food products. With a growing population and with increasing amounts of land planted in cotton, Egypt could no longer feed itself.

An expansion of the transportation and communications network followed on the advances in agriculture, especially from the need to move the cotton crop from the fields to textile factories in Europe. Harbor facilities at Alexandria were modernized. Railroads were completed connecting all the major cities of the Egyptian delta and from Cairo up the Nile into Upper Egypt. Light railways were also established in the delta, and these brought more isolated rural areas into touch with urban centers. The railroads immensely facilitated the transformation of the Egyptian agricultural economy from subsistence farming to cultivation of cash crops. Greater exchange of goods between rural and urban areas followed the breakdown of economic self-sufficiency.

These areas of intensive development must be compared, however, with other spheres of neglect and even regression. The British did little to stimulate Egyptian industrial development. Cromer was an advocate of free trade, believing that countries should specialize economically and exchange the products of their specialization. Of course, in his vision of the world countries like Egypt and India were to be producers of raw materials for the factories of England and the rest of Europe. The consul-general also realized full well the opposition he would encounter from English industrialists if he were to favor the development of local Egyptian industries. Indeed, on one occasion he did experience the force of this opposition. An attempt by a group of British industrialists to establish textile mills in Egypt brought forth strong criticisms from the Lancashire textile industrialists. Cromer responded by establishing an excise tax on the manufactured products in Egypt, and the experiment languished.

Nor did the British diminish the preponderance of the European middle class in Egypt's commercial life. European, and particularly English, banking firms, real estate companies, and public utility companies were granted far-reaching concessions during this period. At the same time, only a few Egyptian-run and -financed companies came into existence. European capital accounted for more than 90 per cent of the financing of joint-stock companies operating in Egypt in 1914.

Educational development was also permitted to lag. At no time before 1914 did money appropriated to the ministry of education exceed 5 per cent of the total Egyptian budget. Moreover, the emphases of British rule had important consequences for educational development. In contrast to the policies of Muhammad Ali and Ismail, the British required tuitional charges from students in the government schools. This requirement meant that the Western education offered by these schools was available only to the wealthier classes, and thus tended to reenforce existing class lines rather than break them down. Another important aspect of British policy was the provision of rudimentary education in the vernacular to the mass of the population in the traditional Islamic schools, the *kuttabs*. On several occasions Cromer remarked that even a rudimentary education along traditional lines would make the masses less susceptible to nationalist appeals from the educated elite.

In spite of constant attacks from nationalist critics, the British adopted a conservative attitude toward parliamentary institutions in Egypt. They permitted the existence of advisory councils on the provincial and national levels, but they did not let these bodies have any significant legislative powers. Moreover, they enacted high property qualifications for membership, so that these organs tended to represent a wealthy and, in most respects, conservative segment of Egyptian society.

Finally, the British strengthened the existing social structure and tried to mitigate the disruptive effects of economic change. While professing sympathy for the oppressed Egyptian peasantry, they allowed immense quantities of land to accumulate in the hands of large landholders. Much of the new arable land brought into cultivation by hydraulic improvements was auctioned off to the highest bidders. The new, modernized courts enabled moneylenders and large landholders to dispossess peasants of their land because of chronic indebtedness. Until just before the First World War the few efforts to stem this trend were weak and ineffectual. Indeed, the

Egyptian peasantry was being turned into an agricultural proletariat working on the lands of large landholders. Moreover, the Western-educated Egyptian intelligentsia found it difficult to break through the alliance between the British and landed Egyptian aristocrats. Many were absorbed into the Egyptian government bureaucracy, but top positions were monopolized by English officials. Increasingly this class turned to nationalist agitation in opposition to the British.

Recovered from its setback in the Arabi revolt, nationalism reappeared in Egypt in the two decades before 1914. It was still largely confined to the educated elite, with Western-educated men beginning to assume a dominant position. Its two emphases, the secular nation-state and Islamic nationalism, nonetheless remained, even appearing in disharmony within the same person. Whereas during the Arabi revolt army leaders had been the source of discontent, in this era the movement was dominated by graduates of the law schools. This was quite natural. The army was carefully controlled by the British, while the Egyptian law school was the elite educational institution in Egypt, attracting the country's most ambitious youth. Its graduates were given a more general exposure to the political and cultural values of the West than were the students of the other two schools of engineering and medicine. The law school had a number of French teachers, left from before the occupation, and there was probably some truth in the British charge that these teachers sought to implant radical political ideas in the minds of their students. Graduates of the law school keenly felt the discrimination against Egyptians in top administrative positions. The two most dynamic leaders of the nationalist movement, Mustafa Kamil and Muhammad Farid, were graduates of the school. They had both been destined for careers in government, but felt that they could not achieve their highest aspirations in a British-dominated civil service. Graduates and students of the law school were the first to organize themselves for the purpose of nationalist agitation and the first to boycott their classes as a technique of protest.

Mustafa Kamil, a product of law schools in Egypt and in France, was the undisputed leader of extremist nationalism until his death in 1908. He was a spellbinding orator, equally a master of harangue in Cairo and Alexandria or in France. He seems to have been a sincere exponent of secular nationalism, for he tried to win the favor of Coptic intellectuals and to keep his following from becoming purely Muslim. But there is a great deal of truth in the British charge that

Egyptian nationalists like Mustafa Kamil, no matter how westernized they were themselves, had to invoke the image of Islam in order to galvanize the Egyptian people. Mustafa Kamil was not a profound intellectual, and he did not have sophisticated ideas of nationalism and the nation-state. His real strength lay in his compelling appeal for resistance to British rule, and in this appeal he was willing to employ a variety of means. His goal was an independent Egypt, endowed with parliamentary institutions and rid of British supervision.

While Mustafa Kamil's ideas may not have been novel, the development of the nationalist movement under his leadership deserves attention. The movement was quite small at first, but Mustafa Kamil had important connections in France. As a spokesman for Egyptian nationalism he was attractive to both the left- and right-wing extremes of French politics—the left because of their antiimperialist sentiments, the right because of their intense opposition to British predominance in Egypt. Consequently, in the early part of his career he spent much of his time in France, writing articles in journals, giving speeches, and moving in the company of French diplomats and politicians. His propagandist campaign was directed more toward France than Egypt, and those efforts to enlarge his following in Egypt were mainly designed to prove to the French public that he was, in fact, a legitimate spokesman of Egyptian nationalism. It is probably true that at this stage of Egyptian nationalism there was little else that he could have done. The nationalist movement in Egypt was too weak to concern the British, who were more embarrassed by French diplomatic pressure. Moreover, many nationalists felt there was danger in trying to appeal to a larger following in Egypt. Mustafa Kamil was a representative of the new educated elite, and his goal was to win independence for Egypt and top positions for his own group. To broaden the nationalist base would have meant appealing to other groups in Egypt—urban proletariat and peasantry—and including these groups in the movement. Mustafa Kamil was no social reformer, and he was extremely reluctant to share power or to blend nationalism with programs of far-reaching social reform.

The hope of forcing England out of Egypt through concerted European diplomacy was bound to fail, for the British would not budge, and the French were not in a position to force them out. The Fashoda crisis of 1898, in which the British forced the French to withdraw their claims to the upper Nile basin, was a disappointment to Egyptian nationalists. It was followed by an Anglo-French agreement in 1904 in which France recognized Britain's predominant position in Egypt. Thus, Mustafa Kamil's original policy of directing his appeals to Europe was a failure, and there was only one way left—to turn to the Egyptian people themselves for support and resistance against British rule. The beginnings of this transformation in Egyptian nationalism were made in the latter years of Mustafa Kamil's career. In 1900 he founded an Arabic newspaper, *al-Liwa*, to popularize nationalist ideals. This paper was reported to have had a circulation of ten thousand during its best years and was clearly regarded by the British as a threat. Efforts were made at the same time to organize under nationalist auspices the students and alumni of the secondary and higher schools. In 1907, in reaction to the creation of other Egyptian political parties, the extreme nationalists also organized their own party, known as *al-Hizb al-Watani* (National Party), which, although possessing the same name as the party created by Ahmad Arabi, was entirely unconnected with it. Arabi's party had disappeared with the crushing of the Arabi revolt.

Mustafa Kamil's death in 1908 did not slow the extension of the nationalist movement. Although his successor, Muhammad Farid, was a less dynamic leader, in many respects he and others in the party added new dimensions to the movement. There were increased efforts to appeal to groups other than the Western-educated and to embrace social reform in conjunction with nationalist appeals. Leaders of the National Party began to penetrate embryonic Egyptian trade unions, and some of the more preceptive leaders saw the virtue of appealing to Egypt's peasant class. With new developments in organization came the introduction of new techniques of resistance. Student boycotts of classes and public demonstrations continued, but already a more radical fringe of political revolutionaries was considering the use of terror and assassination. Although political violence was not yet widespread, one important Egyptian minister was assassinated before 1914, and several other attempts were thwarted by the authorities: the background for the wave of assassinations and terrorism that swept Egypt after World War I. More moderate nationalists were also thinking about techniques of nonviolent resistance and boycott.

Nationalist sentiment was immensely accelerated by World War I, when Britain's capacity to resist nationalist demands was reduced by wartime exhaustion. The result was widespread political rioting and agitation from 1919 to 1924. Early in the war the British took several measures which were deeply resented by Egyptians. The British felt that the old, undefined relationship of Britain to Egypt could not remain unaltered, especially since the Ottoman empire had come into the war on the side of Germany and Austria and was calling on all Muslims to join in a holy war against the British and French. The British broke Egypt's ties with the Ottoman empire and declared a British protectorate over the country. This step drew bitter criticism from Egyptians who felt that the British had merely used the pretext of war to strengthen their control over the country. Britain's numerous promises of evacuation appeared hollow beside this measure. Moreover, the British deposed Khedive Abbas (1892-1914), who had been a consistent opponent of the British throughout his reign. Both actions offended the sensitivities of educated Egyptians.

At the outbreak of the war the British issued a formal statement that they would guarantee the security of Egypt from aggression and that the country would not be called upon to bear extra burdens because of war. This promise was violated almost immediately. The Ottoman attack on the Suez Canal compelled Britain to seek Egyptian assistance, and the Egyptian army was called to serve. Egyptian auxiliary and labor corps were created to support the British forces in the Middle East, and *fellahin* were recruited into these organizations. When the British launched their military campaign into Palestine, Egyptians were recruited in even greater numbers. Casualties were not high in the labor companies which usually worked and lived behind the front lines. But this was not the case in some of the auxiliary corps, particularly the camel transport corps, which followed close on the heels of the fighting units and had many casualties. The British requisitioned Egyptian animals, especially camels, for their desert campaigns. The method of recruiting added to the harshness of the system. Local Egyptian government officials were allowed to collect the recruits, and they used their powers in the most arbitrary fashion. The Egyptian *fellahin*, of course, bore the brunt of this burden. "No fellahin joined [the auxiliary companies] from desire to save his country from invasion and no educated Egyptian ever served in their ranks." [3] Added to these problems was the fact that Britain turned Egypt into a military headquarters for the Middle

[3] P. G. Elgood, *Egypt and the Army* (Oxford: 1924).

East. In 1916, when the British transferred the bulk of the Mediterranean Expeditionary Force withdrawn from Gallipoli to the Suez Canal, there were no fewer than three complete army corps in Egypt. Although numerous Egyptians prospered by supplying British needs, this situation led to friction and hostility between the military and the Egyptian civilian community. The slowness with which Britain demilitarized their forces in Egypt at the conclusion of the war and their continued application of martial law in Egypt intensified resentment.

The economic consequences of war also had a powerful impact on Egypt. By and large the substantial landholders benefited from the wartime inflation. They controlled the cotton farming and were able to sell their crops at inflated prices. The peasantry, on the other hand, suffered the heavy burden of higher prices for foodstuffs and other consumer products. There can be no doubt that the economic and military grievances of the Egyptian peasantry made them ripe for rebellion.

These grievances, however, might have been borne with customary Egyptian endurance had it not been for the ideological currents galvanizing Egypt's educated elite into action. The moral and ideological doctrines of Woodrow Wilson, although designed for European consumption, had great impact on the non-European world. No concept had a greater attraction than national self-determination, each nation independent and free to choose its own destiny. Egyptian intellectuals began to consider the application of these ideas in their own country. Even before the end of the war in 1918 an Egyptian prince, Umar Tussun, brought up the idea of creating an Egyptian committee to present the aspirations of his country to the forthcoming peace conference. In November 1918 Amin al-Rafii sent off a political memorandum to the leaders at Paris presenting the nationalist position. Egyptian intellectuals looked to President Wilson of the United States to champion their interests against the British.

In late 1918 a group of Egyptian leaders under Saad Zaghlul presented demands to Reginald Wingate, the British high commissioner in Egypt. None of these Egyptians was an extreme nationalist or belonged to the National Party, most of whose members had been exiled during the war. Their ties were, in fact, with a more conservative party, representative of the landed and monied interests, known as the Umma Party. Their program was hardly radical. In fact, they began their conversations with the high commissioner with complaints about press censorship and martial law. It was Wingate, in anger, who first introduced into the talks the subject of political independence for Egypt. What the Egyptian Wafd (delegation) wanted at this time was abolition of protectorate status, an end of martial law and press censorship, and some statement about Egyptian independence. They were prepared to give the British certain special privileges, including the garrisoning of troops in the Suez Canal zone for defensive purposes and the appointment of a British adviser to the ministry of finance. And they were purposely vague about the political future of the Sudan. They requested permission to travel to London and Paris to put their demands before diplomats of the major powers. These requests were all denied, and when the Wafd showed itself adamant, the British exiled Zaghlul and three other Wafdists to Malta. This action proved a great blunder, for it sparked rebellion for which the British were not prepared. The rebellion spread out from the urban centers into rural Egypt. Students, civil servants, professional men, and the urban proletariat joined in. Just how politically conscious the rural inhabitants were is difficult to determine. Their rebellion was in part a traditional protest against an oppressive and weakened central government, a type of rebellion familiar in Egyptian history. Much of their activity was directed against the hated Egyptian government officials who had made their lives so miserable during the war. But their actions were closely coordinated, both in time and intensity, with those of the urban areas. In a few villages the peasants, in cooperation with intellectuals, proclaimed short-lived republics. This coordination suggests the work of urban agitators utilizing peasant discontent for nationalist purposes. In the cities nationalist protest took the form of student boycotts and demonstrations and sympathetic strikes by proletariat and professional men alike. The rural areas tended to turn against all symbols of central control, killing representatives of the government, tearing up railway lines, cutting telephone and telegraph lines, and in general isolating themselves from the authority of the central government.

The exile of Wafdist leaders having misfired, the British sought to negotiate and compromise with Egyptian leaders in order to end rebellion and to put their relationship on a firmer basis. The details of these negotiations cannot be presented here. Two salient features emerged from the troubled years 1919 to 1924. The first was the British intention to play a lesser role in internal Egyptian affairs, confining their efforts to securing their strategic and imperial interests in the country. This change in policy meant that Egyptians were to be permitted to run most of the ministries, except the ministries of finance and justice, which the British regarded as impinging on their own interests. The British army of occupation was to remain, but it was to be used less openly, more to defend Britain's strategic interests in the Canal. And Britain was to abrogate the protectorate status and proclaim the independence of Egypt, subject to the above reservations. This general policy was in keeping with other political arrangements being made in the Middle East. The primary goal was to mask British power, conserve British resources—no longer so elastic—define precisely British interests in the Middle East area, and limit the use of British power to the protection of these interests alone.

The second feature was the fact that the British demands, even in the restricted form presented, were not acceptable to Egypt's most popular party, the Wafd. It need not be assumed that the Wafd were the representatives of extremist nationalism. This role was still played by the National Party—although it had lost much of its former popularity—which called for the complete and unfettered independence of Egypt and no negotiations before the withdrawal of British troops. What the Wafd objected to was the garrisoning of British troops in Egypt proper rather than on the east bank of the Suez Canal, which would have been acceptable to them. Its leaders also wanted to terminate or limit the influence of British advisers in the Egyptian government. The Sudan was another point of contention, for Egypt wanted its own sovereignty over the Sudan made clear, while the British were bent upon limiting Egypt's role in that region. So long as the Wafd was the popular party in Egypt, and so long as the Wafd and the British could not agree, there was only one alternative for the British to pursue: the unilateral imposition of their will on the country. Thus, in 1922 the British declared Egypt independent, reserving to itself four significant powers: imperial communications, Egyptian defense, protection of minorities and foreign interests, and hegemony over the Sudan. Then in 1923 a constituent assembly established by the king declared a new parliamentary system in Egypt. Although Egypt's constitution was quite an advanced and liberal one, it is significant that parliamentary government was imposed from the top and not negotiated through the Wafd or confirmed by popular vote.

The three decades from 1925 until the Egyptian revolution of 1952 have often been described as an era of corruption, misgovernment, political turmoil, and loss of purpose and vitality. There can be no question of the troubled nature of these years, but this period can also be viewed as one of uneven development, of growth, partially arrested, which was then to burst forth once a ruling elite had been swept from power. The source of the Egyptian revolution was to be found in these years, not only in the impediments to change, but also in crucial areas of reform and development.

In the political sphere this era was marked by a decline in Wafdist popularity, the rise of sociopolitical groups outside the parliamentary framework which were resolved to overthrow existing political institutions, and a growing disillusionment with parliamentary government. The Wafd had stood at the pinnacle of its prestige and power following the revolution of 1919. In all free elections held until the Secord World War it was always returned overwhelmingly as the majority party in parliament, but its energies and leadership were constantly sapped by resistance from the king, from privileged groups in Egypt, and from the British. At various times in this period elections were rigged, the constitution was altered, and the country was governed without parliament at all. These steps were taken with the active support of the king and the more discreet assistance of the British. Other political parties were founded which represented landed wealth and the interests of finance and industrial capitalism. The industrialists and finance capitalists of Egypt were a small yet influential group. They were tied closely to European capitalists and tended to be conservative in political affairs. They sought cooperation with the British, often in opposition to the Wafd.

Moreover, while encountering this formidable resistance, the Wafd experienced internal conflicts. Many of the men who now governed in support of the king had, in fact, been Wafdists and had broken from the party because of the attractions of political power. On two significant occasions the Wafd sought to make accommodations with the British, and for these concessions they incurred the enmity of the more militant nationalist groups. The first was the

Anglo-Egyptian treaty of 1936, signed under the pressure of growing Italian military activity in the Middle East. The Wafd apparently feared that in case of war in the Middle East, Britain would treat Egypt as a virtual colony, as it had done in the First World War, unless major points of conflict were resolved. Although they won for Egypt an abolition of special privileges for foreigners, Egypt's entry into the League of Nations, and the confinement of British troops in Egypt to the Suez Canal base, they did permit and sanction the continuance of British troops on Egyptian soil and British control of most aspects of Egypt's foreign relations. Again in 1942, while German forces were pushing British troops back into Egypt, the Wafd agreed to take over the Egyptian government and to assist in suppressing rebellious activities against the British.

Increasingly, the Wafd was losing its place as champion of Egyptian nationalism and becoming a party of the privileged landed aristocracy, guarding its privileges against middle and lower class elements. During the disturbance of 1919 to 1924 the Wafd was quite generally supported in the country. But when the party failed to enact impressive social legislation, and when lower class elements began to organize themselves more effectively in trade unions and other sociopolitical groupings, the people were less inclined to throw their support behind a party whose leadership was drawn from landed wealth and upper segments of the educated. Even at the height of its powers, the Wafd had not supported a comprehensive revolutionary program. Its emphasis lay in political opposition to the British and its demand for political independence. It did not seek to transform Egyptian social structure. Wafdists did not favor land redistribution, nor did they ever attack the privileged position of the industrial and finance capitalists. Moreover, as the Wafd became a party of privilege, it began to use the government more blatantly to champion the interests of its own members at the expense of the rest of Egyptian society. The men most committed to making the Wafd into a national party were gradually removed from the party or resigned in protest. Perhaps the most significant illustration of this kind was the resignation of Makram Ubayd in protest against legislation designed to distribute bonuses and emoluments among government supporters of the Wafd. Makram Ubayd's bitter denunciation of corruption in the Wafd, the famous *Black Book*, was an accurate picture of the party's growing corruption and loss of idealism.

Accompanying the decline of the Wafd was the emergence of new political groupings of hitherto unrepresented segments of the Egyptian population. The most influential were the Muslim Brotherhood and Young Egypt. These groups made great efforts to penetrate the lower rungs of the civil service, the graduates of primary and secondary schools who had not gone on to higher education, the urban proletariat, trade unions, and even the peasantry. They were openly contemptuous of parliamentary government. Young Egypt wanted a fascist state; the Muslim Brothers wanted a communal state run on Islamic lines. They regarded Egypt's parliamentary government as the government of the privileged against the rest and as a divisive element in the country. Both of these organizations possessed paramilitary organs and employed terror and assassination. Indeed, nearly all of the political parties in Egypt had paramilitary bodies. Consequently, a great deal of political activity occurred outside the bounds of parliament, in fact in open defiance of it, and was punctuated with considerable political violence.

Undoubtedly the most powerful of the extraparliamentary groups was the Muslim Brotherhood. Its founder, Hasan al-Banna, was a devout Muslim who had been educated in Muslim schools and then at Dar al-Ulum, the teacher training school for Arabic and Islamic subjects. He knew no European language, nor had he been educated in any of the modern Western knowledge. In a certain sense he was the spokesman for those who like himself had little or no specialized Western training but who were eager to recapture their place of prestige in a changing Egyptian society. He disliked Western influence in Egypt. He was especially appalled at the degree of westernization of Cairo and the decline of Islamic values among its educated citizens. Urban centers like Cairo and Alexandria, where Western influence was so strong, were always special objects of attack for the Muslim Brothers. Following his graduation from Dar al-Ulum, Hasan al-Banna was sent to Ismailia as a teacher in a Muslim school. A more appropriate place for quickening his thinking and his resentments against the West could hardly have been found. Ismailia was a canal city, and there, in the form of the Suez Canal Company and garrisons of British troops, Hasan al-Banna came to appreciate the full force of Europe's position in Egypt. He also observed the vast disparities between the wealth of the European community and the poverty of most Egyptians. He spoke his mind frequently on these subjects among his friends and soon gained recognition for himself

as a strong Muslim. In 1928 he was encouraged by friends and ad-
mirers to found an Islamic study and action group, which eventually
grew into the Muslim Brotherhood.

Hasan al-Banna was an expert orator and a dynamic organizer.
Before long his Muslim Brotherhood had branch organizations in
nearly all the major cities and many of the villages of Egypt. At the
height of its popularity the society was said to number 500,000 active
members and even more sympathizers. Supporters were drawn from
all segments of society—the civil service, army, urban population,
student groups, and peasantry—but the hard core seem to have been
men like Hasan al-Banna who suffered disabilities because they were
not in the westernized mainstream of Egyptian modernization. A
secret organ was established and trained for military and terrorist
activity, and this organ carried out the assassinations of several leading Egyptian ministers.

The real power of Hasan al-Banna's ideology lay in its criticism of
Egyptian society. Western influence was attacked. The corruption in
parliamentary life and the palace was ridiculed. The society called
for a new sense of unity based on Islamic principles and designed to
rid the country of Western rule and influence. There was considerable social content in the program of the Brothers, for they favored
cooperative organizations, the founding of local industries, the better
division of wealth, and education for the mass of the population.
Their program, on the whole, was a mixture of reactionary and progressive elements. Their ultimate goal was the creation of an Islamic
order dominated by the religious law, purged of its impure elements.
Hasan al-Banna regarded class antagonism as a sign of the breakdown
of Islamic unity. He favored the abolition of usury, nationalization
of natural resources, expulsion of foreign capital, and promotion of
harmonious labor-management relations within an Islamic framework. On other important issues of modernity, such as the status of
women, the use of Arabic in schools in place of European languages,
and the teaching of Western science, the Muslim Brothers tended to
be more conservative than others.

The continuing vigor of the Muslim Brothers rested heavily on the
leadership and spirit infused into the organization by its founder,
but the pervasive climate of terrorism, much of which had been
unleashed by the Muslim Brothers themselves, eventually engulfed
Hasan al-Banna, who was assassinated in 1949. His successor, Hasan
al-Hudaybi, was less effective, and the movement faltered under his

leadership, splitting into factions. The order was eventually suppressed by the Nasser government, although there is recent evidence to indicate it is enjoying new popularity today.

In the decades before the Nasser revolution of 1952 there was a considerable development of the Egyptian economy. Indeed, it was in this period that Egyptians for the first time entered the industrial and commercial spheres on a large scale. The two world wars were enormous accelerators of economic and social change. European manufactured products could not be exported to Egypt. Capital was not forthcoming, for all the resources of the powerful industrial nations of Europe were absorbed by the war effort. Egypt was thrown back on its own resources and forced to develop its own industrial skills and mobilize its own supplies of capital. At the conclusion of the First World War Egyptian industry and banking were given a much needed boost by one of the country's most resourceful entrepreneurs, Talat Harb. He helped to found a number of Egyptian-run and Egyptian-financed banking institutions, and then with the capital available through these institutions he launched Egyptian industries and transportation companies. The most successful industries were the textile factories. Two huge industrial complexes were established at Mahallah al-Kubra and Kafr al-Dawar, with the most modern equipment for textile manufacturing. These efforts immensely diversified the Egyptian economy, gave it new sources of wealth and new avenues of development, and called into existence at least a rudimentary Egyptian middle class element.

Finance and industrial capitalism was heavily monopolistic. The Misr group, founded by Talat Harb, was easily the most important capitalistic organization, and its directors controlled Egyptian aviation, printing, cinema, textiles, marine transportation, and many other enterprises. The upper middle classes tended to be a conservative political force, and it founded political parties in an effort to draw support and popularity away from the Wafd. Indeed, the president of the Egyptian Federation of Industries, Ismail Sidqi, abolished the Egyptian constitution of 1923 when he was in power in the 1930s.

Industrialization meant the emergence of a modern Egyptian working force. Although it was always small in proportion to the total population, its influence was much greater than sheer numbers would indicate. The first unions in Egypt were created by European workmen who had migrated to that country. Before the outbreak of the

First World War Egyptians created their own unions, and there were strikes in the tobacco industries and among train workers in Cairo and Alexandria. Communist influences were felt in the unions, for a communist party had been organized in Egypt in 1920. But the party never had a large following, and Egypt's proletariat tended to support nationalist programs or that of the Muslim Brothers.

The picture that emerges from the 1920-50 period is one of a country literally bursting at the seams. Trying to hold it within bounds was a group of landed aristocrats, industrial and finance capitalists, and the monarchy, all of whom monopolized the legitimate channels of political authority. No issue is more revealing of this period than the attitude of the ruling elite toward land redistribution. The trend toward the accumulation of large estates in the hands of the wealthy had continued unabated, as had the general impoverishment of the peasant class. Despite increasing expressions of resentment in the press and among Egyptian intellectuals, even the most conservative programs to redistribute land were defeated in Parliament by reactionary landholders. One such program limiting only the new land that could be acquired by proprietors who already owned one hundred acres or more was set aside. Thus, Egypt's parliamentary and traditional leaders were being discredited, while far-reaching social, economic, and political changes were taking place beyond their control.

The movement away from liberal and Western values may also be seen in the intellectual sphere. Until the First World War Egyptian intellectuals were under the inspiration of European liberalism. The writings of John Stuart Mill and Auguste Comte were the guides to thought, and intellectuals in Egypt generally stressed the virtues of a liberal society: free press, parliamentary institutions, freedom of expression. Islamic modernists sought to reconcile Islam with liberal, Western values. This trend came to an end in the 1920s, however, when there was a strong reassertion of more traditional values by Egyptian intellectuals. The most notable development was the storm of disapproval engendered by traditionalists at the publication of two works carrying further the liberal reinterpretation of Islam. One was Abd al-Raziq's *al-Islam wa Usul al-Hukm* (1925), in which it was argued that Islam was a spiritual community and a code of religious precepts binding upon the conscience but having no relationship to politics. Muhammad, the author argued, had not envisaged the establishment of specific political organs. The second work was Taha Husayn's *Fi al-Shir al-Jahili*, noteworthy because of the method of scientific inquiry into pre-Islamic poetry and the author's denial of certain facts asserted in the Koran. These works were in the mainstream of previous liberal, secularist thinking about Egypt and Islam, but in the changing atmosphere of Egypt in the 1920s they were severely censured. Abd al-Raziq was stripped of his position as an Islamic scholar (*alim*), while Taha Husayn was forced to recant and admit that some of the more controversial passages in his book were written in error. Following these events Egyptian intellectuals tended to be less critical of Islam, and even became its apologists. There was also a growing disillusionment with liberal nationalism and with parliamentary institutions. A new emphasis on the virtues of communal organization, the use of nonparliamentary channels for the realization of political goals, appeared.

The Sudan: Mahdiya and Condominium

Five months after the fall of Khartoum the Mahdi suddenly died on June 22, 1885. He left behind a revolutionary movement in the full flush of victory, in which rival Sudanese groups had been momentarily united under his banner to drive out the Turk and to reform Islam. Now the leader was dead, and the competition between his followers, which had hitherto been submerged in the campaigns against the Egyptian administration, boiled up to the surface and threatened to dissolve the Mahdist state. The most sophisticated and cultured of the contenders were the composite of riverine peoples known as the Awlad al-balad (cultivators, villagers) who sought to secure control of the Mahdist state by rallying under the leadership of Muhammad Sharif ibn Hamid and the Ashraf. The Ashraf were the collective relatives of the Mahdi who, like relations in any society, sought to benefit through the position of their kinsman. Their arrogant behavior and subtle attempts to insinuate their way into powerful offices had infuriated the Mahdi. At one point he had publicly denounced them, but upon his death the Ashraf still retained their privileged place in the Mahdist state, to the continuance of which they believed themselves entitled by their relationship to the Mahdi. This claim was all the more significant when backed by the Awlad al-balad with whom the Ashraf were associated by family, tribal, and cultural ties. But if the Awlad al-balad and the Ashraf had claims of family and position, a second, more vigorous group, the Baqqara, were more forceful. The Baqqara had formed the shock troops of the Mahdist armies, and these rough and ready nomads were not prepared to see the fruits of victory snatched from them by the more sophisticated, sedentary riverine villagers. Led by the Khalifa Abd Allahi, the Baqqara troops were stationed principally around Omdurman at the time of the Mahdi's death, and at the great Council of Notables called to appoint the Mahdi's successor they firmly supported Abd Allahi's candidature. With their own troops scattered throughout the Sudan, the Awlad al-balad simply could not force the appointment of Muhammad Sharif. Abd Allahi was thus chosen the successor to the Mahdi. The notables swore allegiance to him (the *bay'a*, a covenant administered as an oath by which one swears spiritual as well as political loyalty to the leader), and he took the title conferred upon him by the Mahdi, Khalifat al-Siddiq. He then set out to consolidate his position against the Awlad al-balad and the Ashraf who were plotting against him.

Throughout the struggle for control of the Mahdist state, and later during subsequent rivalries, a third group played an important role in preventing the Sudan from dissolving into civil war. The holy men who had followed the Mahdi were influential and respected, if not numerically powerful. As befitted their occupations, they had few political ambitions and could hardly have contested with any success against the power of the Baqqara or the Awlad al-balad. Yet these pious men played a vital role in the Mahdist state as mediators in the bitter disputes of the other two rival groups.

The Khalifa's first task was to secure his own precarious position. No sooner had Abd Allahi been declared the Mahdi's successor than the Ashraf sought to depose him, and they were not without the resources to do so. Possessing the overwhelming support of the Awlad al-balad and controlling many influential offices of state as well as the outlying provinces, the Ashraf lacked only a powerful military force in Omdurman itself to overcome Baqqara superiority. Thus, they sought to bring the army of Muhammad Khalid from Darfur to the Nile and force the Khalifa's abdication. During the ensuing months of intrigue the Khalifa proved his ability to rule by the decisive manner in which he frustrated the Ashraf conspiracy. He first secured the Gezira, the principal granary of the Sudan. Then he disarmed the personal retinues of his leading rivals in Omdurman and sent his most trusted officer, Hamdan Abu Anja, to intercept the army of Muhammad Khalid marching from Darfur. Hamdan

Abu Anja was able to arrange the peaceful surrender of Khalid's forces in April 1886, and the conspiracy collapsed. The power of the Ashraf and the Awlad al-balad was quickly circumscribed, and their commanders and officials were soon replaced in the offices of Mahdist state by Baqqara loyal to Abd Allahi. Sullenly hostile, but powerless to challenge Abd Allahi's rule, the dissidents were, however, by no means broken and continued to lurk on the sidelines awaiting an opportunity to seize control of the state.

The driving force of the Mahdiya had been the *jihad*, holy war, to drive out the Turks and to reform Islam. The Mahdi had never meant his revolutionary movement to stop at the borders of the Sudan, and the Khalifa, once he had curtailed the threats to his rule, sought to accomplish the Mahdi's dream of a universal *jihad*. With a zeal compounded from a genuine wish to carry out religious reform, a desire for military victory and personal power, and an appalling ignorance of the world beyond the Sudan, the forces of the Khalifa marched to the four points of the compass to spread Mahdism and extend the domains of the Mahdist State.

In the west, in Darfur, the Khalifa was faced with an attempt by the Fur to regain their independence lost to the forces of al-Zubayr on the battlefield of Al Manawashi in 1874. The Mahdist troops defeated the Fur but were at once confronted by an even greater threat. A religious mystic called Abu Jummayza who claimed magical powers suddenly emerged to give the Fur separatist movement a messianic character. Rallied by his preaching and exhortation, the Fur pressed back the Mahdists and might have driven them from the province had not Abu Jummayza suddenly died, and the inspiration he infused in the Fur vanished with him. Without his leadership the Fur were no match for the Mahdist army of Mahmud Ahmad, who reestablished Mahdist control in Darfur, but for years afterward Mahmud was so preoccupied with sporadic but futile outbreaks against Mahdist rule that he was unable to carry the *jihad* further west.

Just as the *jihad* in the west can be interpreted as a campaign against Fur separatism, so too the *jihad* in the east against the Ethiopian Christians can be construed as a continuation of the endemic hostility between the peoples from the lowland plains of the middle Nile Valley and those inhabiting the lofty heights of the Ethiopian plateau. Neither the Khalifa nor King John of Ethiopia was the kind of man who could ignore a military challenge or an opportunity to take advantage of another's weakness. The result was a desultory and indecisive campaign. The Mahdists were badly beaten in 1887, and to repair their loss Hamdan Abu Anja directed a brilliant campaign which took the Mahdists all the way to the Ethiopian capital at Gondar before retiring. In 1889 the Mahdists launched yet another campaign, only to be momentarily checked at Al Qallabat. Then a chance bullet killed King John, throwing the Ethiopians into panic and resulting in their disastrous defeat. Without the firm hand of King John, Ethiopia dissolved into anarchy, providing the European powers, particularly Italy, with an opportunity to intervene in Ethiopian affairs. As for the fighting between the Mahdists and the Ethiopians, the only lasting result of their indecisive frontier wars was the realization by the Ethiopians that they cannot long live on the hot, malarial plains of the Nile tributaries and the realization by the Sudanese that their constitutions are ill-suited to the uplands of Ethiopia. Since Al Qallabat, the Sudanese and Ethiopians have respected the implacable facts of geography, and peace has prevailed on the frontier, marred only by the occasional border foray, surreptitious slave smuggling, or infrequent commercial dispute.

If the wars in the west and in the east can be regarded as wars of pacification, the extension of the *jihad* northward into Egypt can be interpreted as a legacy of the Mahdi's dream to conquer and reform all the lands and peoples of the Muslim world. Yet the religious inspiration of this campaign was from the beginning compromised by the more sordid, if practical, motives of the Khalifa. Although he could hardly have forgotten the Mahdi's warnings to the Egyptians that he would cleanse the country of corruption, the Khalifa never appears to have had his heart in the Egyptian campaign. Rather, he used the excuse of the *jihad*, just as he later was to use his campaigns in the Southern Sudan, to eliminate officers and men whom he did not fully trust. Thus, the *jihad* in the north was fought mainly by units of the Awlad al-balad and was commanded by the most able military leader the riverine tribes had produced, Abd al-Rahman al-Nujumi. Moreover, the Khalifa failed to support the expedition with proper arms, equipment, and supplies, yet he insisted that al-Nujumi march against the well equipped Anglo-Egyptian forces who defended Egypt's southern frontier at Wadi Halfa under General Grenfell. In spite of their desperate condition the Mahdist forces advanced northward from Dunqula with a loyalty to the Mahdiya which the Khalifa ill deserved. On August 3, 1889,

near the village of Tushki, the Ansar met the forces of General Grenfell and were destroyed. Al-Nujumi was carried from the field mor-
tally wounded. For the first time the Mahdists experienced the
power of British technology and military organization, and thereafter
the presence of Anglo-Egyptian technical superiority loomed on the
northern horizon as a constant concern to the Khalifa and an ominous threat to the Mahdist state.

Finally, the expansionist drive of Mahdism carried the Ansar up
the Nile and into the Southern Sudan. In October 1888 the Khalifa
sent the first of several expeditions to the Southern Sudan. As on the
other frontiers, a combination of motives determined his policy to
acquire the equatorial regions for the Mahdist state. On the one
hand, he was continuing the campaign of Karam Allah Muhammad
Kurqusawi, who had captured the Bahr al-Ghazal in 1884 and had
pressed on into Equatoria, only to be recalled in 1885 at the death
of the Mahdi. The Khalifa now wanted to complete the task of
destroying the last vestiges of Egyptian administration in the Sudan,
represented by the intrepid figure of Emin Pasha and his garrisons
huddled along the Nile. On the other hand, he was extending the
jihad southward in order to spread Islam among the African, Negroid
population, in the process of which he hoped to acquire new recruits
for his slave battalions as well as ivory and other booty. Under the
leadership of Umar Salih the Mahdists drove the Egyptian garrisons
south to Wadelai and Lake Albert, where mutiny and divided leadership rendered them impotent. Here Emin Pasha and those followers still loyal to him were found by a relief expedition led by Henry
Morton Stanley and escorted to the coast. The Mahdists would
almost certainly have destroyed this beleaguered remnant of the
Egyptian administration in Equatoria and pushed on south into the
kingdoms of the interlacustrine Bantu had they not been forced to
turn west to face the advancing forces of Leopold II, king of the
Belgians and sovereign of the Congo Free State. The appearance of
the Congolese on the upper Nile was the first overt attempt by a
European power to challenge the integrity of the Mahdist state,
and the Khalifa responded by sending reinforcements to the south,
consisting usually of those he did not fully trust and wished to exile
from Omdurman. For nearly a decade the Mahdists and the Congolese struggled for control of the upper Nile, until the Ansar were
decisively defeated at Rajjaf in 1897 and in the following year fled

from the Southern Sudan. Although the Mahdist occupation of Equatoria was short-lived, their determination to spread Islam, by fire and sword if necessary, only increased the bitterness of Southern Sudanese toward the Northerners. To the Negroid peoples of the Southern Sudan there was little difference between the Turks and the Mahdists, both of whom represented maltreatment and oppression. In Equatoria the hostile attitude towards the invaders which had been formed during the Turkiya only hardened under the Mahdists.

By 1889 the expansionist spirit of the Mahdist state seemed spent. The unstable occupation of Darfur, the indecisive victory at Al Qallabat, the defeat at Tushki, and Umar Salih's inconclusive campaign in Equatoria were all the Khalifa had to show for the *jihad*. Having squandered the resources of the Sudan on its frontiers, the Mahdist state had reached the limits of its expansion. The *jihad* was abandoned, and a period of consolidation and contraction set in, necessitated by a sequence of bad harvests resulting in famine, epidemic, and death. From 1889 to 1892 the Sudan suffered its most devastating and terrible years as the Sudanese sought to survive on their shriveled crops and emaciated herds. The Khalifa could do nothing to change the weather and, without outside help, could hardly be expected to relieve the hunger. But if he was powerless to change the circumstances of nature, he need not have exacerbated the difficulties of the Sudanese by commanding his Baqqara tribesmen to abandon their homelands in Kordofan and Darfur to join him in Omdurman. The Baqqara were loath to leave their beloved plains, but they obeyed and came. The motives of the Khalifa are clear. He wished to associate the unruly Baqqara more closely with his regime and convert them into a tribal standing army which would defend him against the machinations of the Awlad al-balad and the Ashraf, whom he deeply distrusted. Although the Baqqara were loyal to the Khalifa, their migration was a disaster for the Sudan. Unproductive, the Baqqara devoted their time to devouring the scanty supplies of grain. Moreover, the Khalifa gave them a privileged position, and the Baqqara, wild and illiterate nomads, used that position to treat the more sophisticated and cultured riverine peoples with contempt and insolence. The Awlad al-balad bitterly resented the presence of the Baqqara as much for their overbearing manner as for their voracious appetites. The result was a deep rift between the people of the villages and the nomads, which threatened the Khalifa's regime and remains to this day a source of social tension in the modern Sudan.

Perhaps the ignorance and bad manners of the Baqqara might have been overlooked by the Khalifa if they had proved effective instruments of government. To his great disappointment, however, the Baqqara never accustomed themselves to the discipline of government or the routine of settled life. They longed for the wide open spaces of southern Kordofan and Darfur. Many stole away at night. Those who remained became unbearable to the Awlad al-balad, so that by 1891 they and the Ashraf, under the leadership of Muhammad Sharif, occupied strategic areas of Omdurman and sought to depose the Khalifa. As in 1885, Abd Allahi reacted with vigor. He cordoned off the conspirators and negotiated a settlement in return for the arms of the insurgents. Once they were disarmed, however, the Khalifa refused to honor his pledges and proceeded to break the power of the Awlad al-balad and the Ashraf once and for all. Their notables were sent into exile at Fashoda, their goods were confiscated, and their leader, Muhammad Sharif, was thrown into prison. Until the end of the Mahdist state the Khalifa no longer had to fear an internal threat to his rule.

After the collapse of the conspiracy of 1891 the Mahdist state entered its halcyon years before the final confrontation with the Anglo-Egyptian forces. After 1892 the harvests improved and food was no longer in such desperately short supply. Moreover, the autocracy of the Khalifa had become acceptable to most Sudanese, even the riverine tribes, for the Khalifa had come to represent that authority to which the Sudanese were not only accustomed but upon which they had come to depend. The need for dependence arose from complex tribal, family, and religious relationships, all of which were interdependent and which the Sudanese accepted, and indeed required, as the normal pattern of living. During the Turkiya the deep-felt need for dependence produced by their traditional way of living was demonstrated by the acceptance of an alien and authoritarian Egyptian regime until the Mahdi presented himself as an autocratic substitute to whom the Sudanese could transfer their dependence and consequently their loyalty. Now, in the quiet years of the Mahdiya when the Khalifa had tempered his own despotism and eliminated the gross defects of his administration, he too received the widespread acceptance, if not devotion, which the Sudanese had accorded the Mahdi. Any attempt by a foreign invader to destroy that authoritarianism, so acceptable and so necessary to the mass of Sudanese, would be strongly resisted and only accepted in turn if an equally authoritarian symbol were to replace that of the Khalifa.

During these years the Khalifa himself appears to have hoped to transform the Mahdiya into an Islamic monarchy. In the true fashion of an oriental potentate, he withdrew from public view and built a great wall around his quarters to seal himself from the people. During this same period he abandoned his reliance on the Baqqara, who had proved intractable, and expanded his bodyguard, the *mulazimiyya*, into a regular standing army of some ten thousand troops. Unlike the early years of the Mahdiya, when a host of military commanders and prominent officials had scrambled for influence, only two other individuals besides the Khalifa were of any importance in the Mahdist state: Yaqub, brother of the Khalifa, and Abd Allahi's son Uthman. Yaqub appears to have been the tough and devoted servant of the regime. He destroyed many officials who aroused his suspicions or who were unfortunate enough to be members of the Awlad al-balad and thereby subject to Yaqub's Baqqara prejudices. Uthman was a striking contrast to his uncle. Well educated and intelligent, his appreciation of culture and breadth of understanding were compromised by a dissolute past which was used against him by his envious rival Yaqub.

For many years the commonly held conception of the Khalifa's rule has been one of unbridled and savage barbarism. Recent scholarship has demonstrated that this was clearly not the case, as the most cursory examination of the Khalifa's administration will make apparent. The Sudan was divided into a metropolitan heartland surrounded by frontier provinces. On the frontiers the administration was in the hands of the military commanders, who possessed an extraordinary amount of autonomy, with control over their own treasuries and even with independent powers of taxation. The metropolitan provinces, on the other hand, were clearly tied to the central government, and the governors of these regions were little more than tax collectors, taking all their orders directly from Omdurman. The administration was also divided along tribal lines, for all the military commanders were Baqqara, while the clerks and collectors were always non-Baqqara, usually from the Awlad al-balad, for illiterate nomads could hardly hope to keep accounts and carry on official correspondence. The Khalifa's reliance on the Baqqara went even further in the frontier provinces, for the military commanders were not only Baqqara but of the Khalifa's own clan, the Jubarat branch of the Taaisha Baqqara. The principal problem of such an organization of administration was to retain control over the frontier governors. The loyalties of tribal and clan affiliation were frequently insufficient to permit the frontier governors a completely free hand, and since the Khalifa never left Omdurman, he relied on commissions of prominent men to investigate the administration of his agents on the borderlands. Such an alternative was not always entirely satisfactory.

The hub of the Mahdist state was Omdurman, which had grown from the Mahdi's camp into a sprawling city. In the center was the walled citadel, enclosing the Khalifa's house, the Mahdi's tomb, the arsenal, storehouse, treasury, and the other institutions of the central government. Within the citadel the machinery of government depended entirely on the Khalifa, whose daily routine consisted of conferences and audiences during which Abd Allahi gave his commands. The social tension between the Awlad al-balad and the Baqqara, which pervaded the Mahdiya, was also present at the innermost circles of the Khalifa's councils, for all the clerks and technicians who made up the central bureaucracy were non-Baqqara and consequently never fully trusted by the Khalifa. In fact, nearly a third of the clerical employees had been officials under the Egyptian regime and thus provided a continuity of administration from Turkiya to Mahdiya.

In spite of its many defects the Khalifa's administration served the Sudan better than its many detractors would admit. Certainly the Khalifa's government was autocratic, but while autocracy may be repugnant to European democrats, it was not only understandable to the Sudanese but appealed to their deepest feelings and attitudes formed by tribe, religion, and past experience with the centralized authoritarianism of the Turks. By restoring order and unity after the death of the Mahdi, the Khalifa successfully provided that symbol of dependence in which the Sudanese could find psychological comfort, if not material satisfaction. For them, the Khalifa was equal to the task of governing bequeathed him by the Mahdi. Only when confronted by new forces from the outside world, of which he was ignorant, did Abd Allahi's abilities fail him. His belief in Mahdism, his reliance on the superb courage and military skill of the Mahdists, and his own ability to rally them against an alien invader were simply insufficient to preserve his independent Islamic state against the overwhelming technological superiority of Great Britain. And as the nineteenth century drew to a close, the rival imperialisms of the European powers brought the full force of this technological supremacy against the Mahdist state.

When the British forces invaded Egypt in 1882, Gladstone's government intended the occupation to be short. Even the Conservatives at first viewed British control at Cairo as a temporary necessity. By 1889, however, Lord Salisbury had come around to the view of his advisers at Cairo, particularly Lord Cromer, that the British must remain in Egypt to prevent the collapse of the Khediviate and the possible intervention of a power hostile to Britain. This was a momentous decision, not only for Britain and Egypt, but for the Sudan as well. If Britain were to continue the task of modernizing Egypt for many long years instead of a few short ones, the defense of the Nile, upon which the very existence of Egypt was directly dependent, became of supreme importance to British policy in northeast Africa. Once Britain had lost control of the upstream tributaries and sources of the Nile, her position in Egypt and at Suez would be irreparably jeopardized. Hitherto the British government had not concerned itself over the Nile waters; the Nile basin was, after 1885, in the hands of the Mahdists, whose primitive technology precluded interference with the life-giving waters. By 1889, however, this distant unconcern had changed to real fears of insecurity. A more permanent occupation of Egypt required the inviolability of the Nile waters, not from any African state, who could hardly have seriously interfered with them, but from rival European powers who could. At first British officials sought to seal off the Nile Valley by diplomacy. In the spring of 1890 Lord Salisbury, the British prime minister, warned the Italians, who had laid claim to Kassala below the Ethiopian escarpment in the Sudan, to keep out of the Nile Valley, and in 1891 the Italians formally agreed to restrict their activities to the Ethiopian highlands. Next Salisbury turned to the Germans, whose most aggressive African explorer, Carl Peters, was marching toward the upper Nile ostensibly to rescue his fellow countryman Emin Pasha. Assisted by an agreement, the Mackinnon Treaty, between the Imperial British East Africa Company and the Congo Free State, Salisbury was able to conclude an arrangement with the German government in 1890, commonly known as the Heligoland Treaty, recognizing a British sphere on the upper Nile. Although the Mackinnon Treaty facilitated Salisbury's agreement with the Germans, it cleared the way, diplomatically, for a Congolese advance to the Nile. By letting the Congolese into the Nile Valley, Salisbury began a dispute with Leopold II over the Southern Sudan which was not to end until 1906. But the Congo Free State in these years was habitually pressed for funds, and although it was to become in the twentieth century an irritating obstacle to British control of the Nile sources, the greatest threat at that time came from France.

The French had always opposed the British occupation of Egypt, as much from the humiliation brought about by their own indecision as for the paramountcy Britain had won at Cairo and Suez. Since the beginning of the British occupation the French had been the most shrill in their demands for a British withdrawal, and French opposition to Britain in Egypt had wide repercussions in the Sudan. In fact, once it became apparent that the British were determined to remain in Egypt, the French immediately began to plot how to get them out. In the spring of 1893 an elaborate plan was concocted by which a French expedition would march through Africa to Fashoda on the upper Nile where the French hydrologist, M. Prompt, believed a dam could be constructed to obstruct the flow of the Nile waters. Although the French mission was suspended because of complications in Europe, the British learned of the expedition and set about to block its path by an agreement with the Congo Free State signed in the spring of 1894. The agreement leased most of the Southern Sudan to King Leopold, conveniently athwart the route the French expedition would have to follow. Unfortunately for the British government, the Anglo-Congolese agreement failed to achieve its object. Both Germany and France put such pressure upon Leopold that he had to abrogate the key articles of the agreement, leaving the way to the Nile free and clear. Eighteen months later instructions were drafted in Paris to send a new expedition to the Nile under Captain Marchand. Marchand set out for Africa in June 1896, having been exhorted to "Go to Fashoda. France is going to fire her pistol." [4]

The French were fortuitously assisted by events in Ethiopia. On March 1, 1896, the Italian army, which had been advancing into

[4] Hanotaux to Marchand, quoted in Général Mangin to Général Des Garets, Fashoda, November 6, 1898, "Lettre de la Mission Marchand," *Revue des Deux Mondes*, September 15, 1931, p. 277.

Ethiopia to secure those wild uplands for the greater glory of the new Italy, was disastrously defeated at Adua by the Ethiopian army under King Menelik. The ultimate effect of the Italian collapse was to open the way for French encroachment westward through Ethiopia toward the Nile in support of Marchand. The immediate effect, however, was an Italian appeal to the British government for a demonstration in the Northern Sudan to relieve their theatened position at Kassala. How a demonstration at Wadi Halfa was to take the pressure off the Italians at Kassala, some seven hundred miles away, remains a mystery known only to the Italian foreign office, but Salisbury was delighted to seize this opportunity to advance into the Sudan and to acquire a permanent gain for Egypt without repercussions in Europe. Under the command of General Sir Herbert Kitchener, the Anglo-Egyptian forces marched southward from Wadi Halfa, defeated the Mahdists in a series of engagements, and occupied Dunqula by September 1896.

The Dunqula campaign had little to do with the Marchand expedition. Kitchener's troops were ordered forward in March 1896, three months before Marchand set out for Africa. The Dunqula campaign was merely obtaining Sudanese territory on the cheap. To Salisbury, however, it soon became apparent that greater expense would have to be incurred to stop the French. As reports reached London during 1896 and 1897 of Marchand's progress in western Africa and French activities in Ethiopia, Britain's inability to insulate the Nile Valley was embarrassingly exposed. Salisbury desperately tried one scheme after another to beat the French to Fashoda. He first sought to accelerate the construction of the Uganda Railway to the Central African Lakes, and when that failed, he sent MacDonald to Uganda with orders to march to Fashoda. MacDonald never accomplished his mission, and by the autumn of 1897 British authorities had come to the reluctant conclusion that the conquest of the Sudan was necessary to protect the Nile waters from French encroachment. In October Salisbury ordered Kitchener to advance up the Nile.

Kitchener had been preparing for the conquest of the Sudan since the end of the Dunqula campaign. A railway was boldly constructed from Wadi Halfa directly across the Nubian desert to Abu Hamad, which was captured in August 1897. The Khalifa was clearly taken by surprise at the power of British technology. He had decided to let the invaders penetrate deep into the Sudan where his massed armies could fall upon them much as the Mahdi had done to Hicks at Shaykan. Consequently, throughout 1897 the Mahdist forces were concentrated at Omdurman, and the great army of Mahmud Ahmad, which had arrived from Darfur, was stationed at Al Matamma, the terminus of the desert route from Dunqula, to defend the Omdurman approaches. To send the Baqqara troops of Mahmud Ahmad to occupy the principal town of the Jaaliyin, one of the most influential tribes of the Awlad al-balad, was a tactless blunder which the Khalifa soon compounded into tragedy by ordering the Jaaliyin to evacuate their town. The Khalifa had never overcome his suspicions of the Awlad al-balad, and he now let his habitual distrust of them jeopardize his own regime. The Jaaliyin were determined not to abandon their town to Mahmud's Baqqara. They rebelled and were promptly massacred by the Ansar. Once again the hatred between the Awlad al-balad and the Baqqara was rekindled by blood, the *jihad* against the invaders was compromised, and another bitter memory was added to the hostility between villager and nomad.

Once given permission to advance, Kitchener pushed steadily but cautiously up the Nile to the Atbara River, where on April 8, 1898, he encountered Mahmud's army. Since the defeat of the Jaaliyin, Mahmud had lain inert at Al Matamma, and when he at last began to move northward in search of Kitchener's army, he could not find supplies for his straggling mass of ill-disciplined and demoralized troops. Hunger may have weakened the Ansar, but it did not diminish their courage. At the Atbara the Mahdists fought with superb bravery, but they were overwhelmed by the superior technology, organization, and discipline of the Anglo-Egyptian troops.

After his victory on the Atbara Kitchener spent four months preparing for the final advance to Omdurman. By now Salisbury was thoroughly alarmed by the French drive to the Nile, and additional British troops, gunboats, and artillery were sent up the Nile to insure the defeat of the Mahdists. While Kitchener prepared to advance, the Khalifa massed an enormous army of some eighty thousand men at Omdurman to overwhelm the infidel invaders in one final battle. Early in the morning of September 2, 1898, the Khalifa hurled his troops at the Anglo-Egyptian defense perimeter which Kitchener had drawn up by the Nile at Iqayqa, six miles north of Omdurman. To the west lay the Karari Hills, and swarming down to the plains at their base came the Ansar, to hurl themselves with matchless but useless courage against Kitchener's machine guns. By midday the Battle of Karari was over. Eleven thousand Ansar lay dead; some sixteen thousand were wounded. Kitchener lost forty-eight killed and 382 wounded.

When he saw that the day was lost, the Khalifa returned to Omdurman to rally his reserves. He failed and rode off with his bodyguard to Kordofan, where he remained a fugitive until November 1899. Then a British force under General Wingate cornered him at Umm Diwaykarat. Once again the machine gun decided the battle. The Khalifa of the Mahdi lay dead upon his sheepskin rug. The Mahdiya had ended.

Five days after the defeat of the Khalifa on the plains of Karari, a steamer filled with Ansar arrived from the south. The Ansar reported that they had been shot at by Europeans, and an examination of the bullets lodged in the steamer showed them to be of French manufacture. Marchand had reached Fashoda. Kitchener acted at once. He opened the special orders given to him by the British government for use if he came across Europeans on the upper Nile. The orders instructed him to contest their claims. With a powerful flotilla Kitchener steamed south to Fashoda, where he met Marchand on September 18. The intrepid French captain refused to withdraw, and Kitchener, rather than shoot down the small French force, referred the matter to London. The long expected Fashoda crisis was on. At first both the French and the British governments refused to give way, and both prepared for war. The French, however, could not fight. Their navy was in deplorable condition. The army was demoralized and weakened by the Dreyfus affair, and Marchand himself could hardly have been supported at his isolated outpost. The French thus gave way, and in the Anglo-French declaration of March 1899 limited French eastern expansion at the Nile watershed. This was a great British diplomatic victory, but it did not entirely secure the Nile basin. Having eliminated the French from the Nile, the British were now confronted by the forces of the Congo Free State. Leopold II had long dreamed of becoming a Nilotic power, and for a decade had expended vast amounts of men and money to establish a foothold on the river. In 1897 his forces had driven the Mahdists from Rajjaf and founded a Congolese post there. Now Leopold revived his legal claims to the Bahr al-Ghazal, which would have given the Congo Free State control of the myriad of Nile sources which rise on the Congo-Nile watershed. Having been prepared to fight a major war to push the French from the

Southern Sudan, the British were not about to hand over the Bahr al-Ghazal to Leopold. Many years of acrimonious negotiations followed, until Leopold finally capitulated in 1906. By 1910 the Nile Basin from its source to its mouth was at last securely British.

Having conquered the Sudan, the British now had to administer it. But the administration of this vast land was complicated by the legal and diplomatic problems which had accompanied the conquest. The Sudan campaigns had been undertaken by the British to protect their imperial position as well as the Nile waters, yet the Egyptian treasury had borne the greater part of the expense, and Egyptian troops had far outnumbered those of Britain in the Anglo-Egyptian army. The British agent in Cairo, Lord Cromer, did not simply want to hand the Sudan over to Egyptian rule, for that would mean the extension to the Sudan of the capitulations, those privileges to Europeans and Americans which had done so much to hamper the task of modernization in Egypt. Moreover, those Englishmen who concerned themselves with such matters were convinced that the Mahdiya was the result of sixty years of oppressive Egyptian rule in the Sudan, and no British government was prepared to hand back the Sudanese to a form of administration against which they had once before revolted. The alternative was, of course, to annex the Sudan outright to the British empire, but this would have been a shocking violation of Egypt's historic claims and her contributions to the river war.

The solution to Britain's dilemma was the Condominium, an ingenious scheme created by Lord Cromer and approved by the Egyptian government in the Anglo-Egyptian agreement of 1899. The Sudan was given a separate political status. Sovereignty was jointly shared by the Khedive and the British Crown; the Egyptian and the British flags were flown side by side. The claims of the Ottoman sultan were ignored, and no European privileges were allowed. Egyptian legislation was not to be applied in the Sudan; rather, the government of the Sudan was invested in a governor-general appointed by the khedive but nominated by the British government. The governor-general was responsible for the complete military and civil organization of government in the Sudan, an authoritarian arrangement with which the Sudanese were well acquainted from past experience. The name *Condominium* was of course bogus. To political theorists joint sovereignty is a contradiction because sovereignty cannot be shared, and in reality there was no equal partnership between Britain and Egypt. From the first Britain dominated the Condominium, leaving the Egyptians with feelings of bitter humiliation at supposedly being maneuvered out of their historic rights by a clever legal agreement. So long as Britain remained in Egypt, the Condominium functioned smoothly, but once in control of their own affairs the Egyptians sought equal partnership in the Sudan. This the British refused to recognize, and from that point the Condominium became a source of embarrassment and friction in Anglo-Egyptian relations.

The principal task facing the Anglo-Egyptian forces after their victory at Karari was the pacification of the plains of the Sudan beyond the rivers. The Khalifa was still at large and had to be hunted down, but of even greater danger were a host of local risings in the Northern Sudan, usually sparked by the preaching of a holy man proclaiming himself to be the Prophet Jesus (al-Nabī 'Isā), or another Mahdi, to drive the infidel out of the Sudan.[5] Indeed, most Sudanese in these early years did not distinguish between the British and the Turks who had previously ruled, referring to the Condominium simply as al-Turkiya al-Thaniya, the second Turkiya. Soon after the Khalifa's death a band of Ansar arose in anticipation of the coming of the Prophet Jesus. In 1903 a Mahdi declared himself in Kordofan, and in 1904 another Jesus appeared at Sinja on the Blue Nile. In 1908 a larger rebellion broke out in the Gezira, led by a former Mahdist amir, Abd al-Qadir Muhammad Imam, known as Wad Habuba, and in 1912 one of his followers established himself as a Prophet Jesus in Kordofan. Some of these rebels were condemned as heretics and exiled. Others were captured, tried, and hung. A few were shot down in hard fought military engagements. Virtually all of these revolts were messianic in character and limited to a few immediate followers of a local holy man. Nevertheless, the persistence of such risings created an obsession with security on the part of British officials that long outlived its cause. Before the outbreak of the First World War these local religious rebellions had become decidedly less frequent and the acceptance of the administration by the Sudanese had increased greatly, yet the administrative policies of the Sudan government remained conditioned by fears of insecurity for many years thereafter.

[5] The appearance of a Mahdi in Muslim eschatology is associated with the second coming of Jesus after the manifestation of the Mahdi. Thus, after the death of Muhammad Ahmad more than one individual proclaimed himself to be the Prophet Jesus.

Only in the Southern Sudan were these fears justified. Before the occupation of the southern provinces could begin, the Nile and its tributaries had to be cleared of matted vegetation called the sadd. By 1901 the river routes to the south had been opened after a herculean effort by hundreds of Mahdist prisoners under the command of Major Peake Bey and his British engineers, but even today it requires great effort to keep the Nile free to navigation by removing the sadd and the more recent but more dangerous water hyacinth each year. Once the river was open, an Anglo-Egyptian expedition was rushed into the Bahr al-Ghazal, as much to frustrate the claims of the Congo Free State as to extend British administration. Here British officers established a network of posts throughout the province and along the Bahr al-Jabal in the former Equatoria Province. But the construction of government posts garrisoned by Sudanese troops and managed by British officials did not mean that the *Pax Britannica* was imposed on the vast reaches of the countryside surrounding the isolated stations. At first the Southern Sudanese regarded the British as just another invader who would undoubtedly attempt to suppress their independence and exploit their human and natural resources. By cajolery, gifts, and peaceful displays of force, and at other times by offers of protection, threats, and even the use of punitive military expeditions, the British officers gradually overcame the Southerners' traditional but justified suspicions of strangers. For the first twenty-five years of British rule in the Southern Sudan the district officials were always military officers seconded from the Egyptian army. Known affectionately throughout the British empire as the "Bog Barons," they remained in the southern provinces, and usually in the same district, for many years, spoke English or an African language rather than Arabic, and closely identified themselves with the people they ruled. They trekked throughout the countryside visiting chiefs, villages, and tribal gatherings. On occasion they were accompanied by a well armed escort, but a lonely district officer tramping through the bush with a butterfly net and a few porters frequently made a greater impression than companies of well disciplined troops. With or without arms, however, the purpose was the same—to establish the authority of the Sudan government, hopefully by peace, but if necessary by war. So long as they kept the peace in their district and spent as little money as possible, the Bog Barons were left alone by the central government, an attitude these officers did nothing to discourage. But this indifference on the part of the central authorities resulted in few attempts at modernization, and a generation was to pass before the handful of British officers could claim that they had unquestioned control throughout the length and breadth of the southern provinces.

Administration in the Northern Sudan was more sophisticated. The aim of the administration in the Muslim Sudan was to modernize, not just pacify. The first governor-general was the conqueror of Karari himself, Lord Kitchener, but in 1899 he left for the South African war, and his former aide Sir Reginald Wingate was appointed to succeed him. As the director of military intelligence of the Egyptian army since 1889, Wingate knew the Sudan and became, during his long tenure as governor-general (1899-1916), devoted to its people and their prosperity. His tolerance and trust in the Sudanese resulted in policies which did much to establish confidence in Christian, British rule by a devoutly Muslim, Arab-oriented people. Moreover, the Sudan in these early years was particularly suited to Wingate's obsession with the most petty problems and the most obscure details, for the Sudan government was small and its problems, though great, never so numerous as to confuse priorities. Only in his later career, when the position of the governor-general changed from that of an office manager to that of a corporation director, did the mass of detail to which he had so long been accustomed confuse the formation of wider policies.

During the Wingate years the Sudan government was advised by the curious figure of Rudolf von Slatin Pasha. Slatin had visited Egypt and the Sudan in 1874, where in Khartoum he had met Eduard Schnitzer, the famous Emin Pasha, who was on his way to join Gordon in Equatoria. Slatin liked the Sudan and asked Emin to recommend him to Gordon. Four years passed, but Gordon did not forget. In July 1878 Slatin was invited to join the Sudan government, and upon completing his military service in Austria he arrived in Khartoum to begin an association with the Sudan that did not end until 1914. In 1881 Slatin was appointed general governor of Darfur, where he tried to stem the tide of Mahdism, failed, turned Muslim, and surrendered to the Mahdists. Thereafter he was servant, slave, and adviser to the Mahdi's successor, the Khalifa, until he escaped from Umdurman to Egypt in 1895. Although his dramatic flight and subsequent bestseller, *Fire and Sword in the Sudan*, made him a romantic and dashing figure to be cultivated by the great and near great, his role in the conquest of the Sudan and the administration of the Condominium was intrinsically more important. In constant attendance on the Khalifa during his captivity, Slatin was privy to the innermost secrets of the Mahdist state, which, after his flight to Egypt, were promptly placed at the disposal of Wingate, the director of military intelligence. The plans of the Anglo-Egyptian conquest were based in no small degree upon Slatin's experience of the Mahdiya. This same knowledge soon proved even more valuable to the newly created Sudan administration. As inspector-general of the Sudan he became the *eminence gris* behind Wingate. Slatin supplied the information, Wingate the policy, and together they fashioned the direction and spirit of the Anglo-Egyptian administration in the Sudan. The professional association was accompanied by an equally deep personal attachment. To Slatin, Wingate was his dear friend Rex. To Wingate, Slatin was good old Rowdy. Slatin repaid Wingate's friendship by introducing him to the great spas of Europe; Wingate responded to Slatin's loyalty by presenting him to English society. This happy and halcyon relationship came abrutly to an end in 1914 when Slatin, torn between his love for the British in the Sudan and his Austrian homeland, resigned from the Sudan service and devoted himself to the work of the Austrian Red Cross.

Perhaps it was just as well, for Slatin appeared charming but a bit old-fashioned to the eager young men who came out from Oxford and Cambridge to modernize the Sudan. Below the governor-general the Sudan was divided into provinces, and each province into districts. Each province was the responsibility of a British governor and each district that of a British officer with an Egyptian or Sudanese *ma'mur* (assistant) and a small clerical staff and police force. At first the governors reported directly to Wingate, but after 1910 the informal meetings of the governor-general's staff were reorganized into a formal council, the principal members being the civil secretary, the legal secretary, and the financial secretary. Thereafter the governor-general, particularly after Wingate's departure, meddled less in the daily administration, deliberately becoming a figure of awe and symbol of authoritarian rule, while the governors reported to the various secretaries. The power of a secretary depended as much on the ability and personality of the individual as on his position within the bureaucracy. By its nature the office of civil secretary was concerned with the execution of internal policy, and under the efficient and brilliant tenure of Sir Harold MacMichael the office of civil secretary became the single most powerful office after that of the governor-general.

At first the British staff consisted of British officers seconded from the Egyptian army, but unlike the Southern Sudan, where military officers remained until the end of the Condominium, civilians were recruited as early as 1900, mostly from Oxford and Cambridge universities, to supplement and to replace military men. These civilian administrators soon evolved into a small elite known as the Sudan political service, which in fact ruled the Sudan as an offshoot of the Sudan civil service, the latter containing the hierarchy of lesser administrative officers and technical personnel. Candidates for the Sudan political service were selected by an interviewing board of members of the Sudan government, who quite naturally tended to choose men in their own image—men of impeccable character with good family connections, sound personality, athletic achievements, and an English public school education. Thus character, health, and prowess on the playing fields were better qualifications for admittance into the service than intellectual ability. Although the need for sound, competent, steady men was clearly most desirable for service in a country like the Sudan, with its taxing climate and lonely spaces, the recruitment of men of similar attainments encouraged conformity rather than creativity, duty rather than initiative, and paternalism rather than tutelage. The service was always small in number, never more than 150 at any one time, and no more than four hundred in the whole history of the Condominium. These administrators were accorded wide latitude in running their districts, another factor which contributed to their *esprit de corps*. But their very confidence, knowledge, and devotion to the Sudanese frequently obscured their judgment and made them slow to react to the new forces which modernization unleashed in the Sudan. In spite of such provincialism—even narrowness—uniformity, and conservatism, the Sudan political service created a viable state from the conglomeration of disparate parts and differing peoples which threatened to disintegrate at the end of the Mahdiya.

Modernization in the Sudan was at first slow. Taxes were purposely kept light, and the Sudan government consequently had few funds available for development. In fact, the Sudan remained dependent for many years on an Egyptian subvention. Nevertheless, vernacular, technical, and primary schools were begun, more to provide the administration with clerks and artisans rather than to instruct the Sudanese in the broader concepts of liberal learning. Economic development depended on communications, and railways, telegraph, and steamer services were expanded, particularly in the Gezira in order to launch the great cotton-growing scheme of that region. Although the war delayed the beginnings of that most spectacular of African agricultural projects, the meticulous planning required for its success took place between 1905 and 1914. During the First World War the Sudan government extended its administration to Darfur, where the autonomous sultan, Ali Dinar, was killed in a brief campaign in 1916; his province was taken over by British administrators, and the final delimitation of the western boundary of the Sudan provided for in the Anglo-French declaration of 1899 was at last completed in 1924.

The First World War itself was a dramatic demonstration of the loyalty of the Sudanese to the Anglo-Egyptian administration. The Sudanese not only ignored the call of the Ottoman Turks to the *jihad* but provided the allies with moral and material support. Among the vast majority of Sudanese, particularly the tribal *shaykhs* of village and steppe, the British officials had built up a great reserve of trust which created political stability in a traditionally volatile land. The Sudan government clearly suited traditional Sudanese society precisely because it was authoritarian and paternal without being oppressive.

One group of Sudanese, however, was gradually drawn away from the traditional political and social framework. These were the Western-educated, middle class elite, who had adopted many ideas and manners from European culture. Under the leadership of Sir James Currie a program of vernacular elementary schools, technical schools, and primary (later called intermediate) schools was implemented to expose a limited number of Sudanese to the rudiments of Western education and to prepare them to serve the government as clerks and artisans. Foremost among the schools was the Gordon Memorial College, opened in 1902 with funds solicited after Kitchener's appeal in 1898 for a suitable memorial to Gordon's name. The college originally consisted of a primary and technical school but later evolved into a secondary school and ultimately into Khartoum University. Educated in these schools to the mysteries of Western technology, and inculcated with the cultural and political values of Western Europe stressing independence and liberal democracy, the new middle class Sudanese, like others elsewhere in the Middle East and Africa, turned less and less to the tribe for inspiration and saw in the British administration that dependence and acceptance of authority they had been taught to reject. Scorned by the British officials, who preferred the illiterate but contented fathers to the ill-educated, rebellious sons, and adrift from their own customary tribal and religious affiliations, these Sudanese turned for encouragement and sympathy to Egyptian nationalists in the Sudan, and from that association Sudanese nationalism in this century was born.

Ironically, the first sputterings of Sudanese nationalism did not derive its inspiration from Egypt. In 1921 Ali Abd al-Latif, a former Dinka army officer who claimed to have been unjustly treated by a British officer, formed the United Tribes Society to work for the independence of the Sudan under its tribal leaders. His exhortations soon led to his arrest in 1922 and brief imprisonment. In 1924 he was back again. This time, however, his rudimentary political ideas had become, under Egyptian tutelage, more subtle. Not only was he prepared to cooperate with the Egyptians, but he formed the White Flag League whose purpose was to drive out the British and establish a united Egypt and Sudan under the Egyptian monarchy. Abd al-Latif's conversion was not simply gross opportunism, for he himself symbolized the basic dilemma of nationalism in the Sudan which later plagued more sophisticated nationalists—an independent Sudan or unity with Egypt. Today it is impossible to assess accurately whether unity with Egypt was, to Sudanese nationalists, merely a political manueuver to embarrass the British or a real commitment to a united Nile Valley. The establishment and apparent success of an independent Sudan today has obscured the embryonic attitudes and feelings of the early nationalists.

In June 1924 the White Flag League demonstrated in Khartoum, and Abd al-Latif was again arrested. In August the cadets of the military school demonstrated in Khartoum and were supported by the mutiny of the Egyptian railway battalion at Atbara. Both these disturbances were firmly suppressed. Although many of the Sudanese elite sympathized with the demonstrations, the country remained quiet. Then suddenly, on November 19, 1924, Sir Lee Stack, the governor-general of the Sudan, by virtue of his office the *sirdar* or commander-in-chief of the Egyptian army, was assassinated in Cairo. The British retaliated with obstinate fury, and Viscount Allenby, the British high commissioner in Egypt, sought to use the incident to end the growing tension between the British and the Egyptians in the Sudan. He demanded that all Egyptian officers and men be withdrawn from the Sudan within twenty-four hours. The Egyptian detachments, at the points of British bayonets, were at once placed on trains and sent down the Nile, but at the same time part of the Eleventh Sudanese Battalion mutinied in sympathy and barricaded themselves in the military hospital in Khartoum. When they refused to surrender, they were annihilated by British artillery. The Sudan government urged the British government in London to terminate the Condominium, but this was too bold a step, and the Condominium continued theoretically in force, though for all practical purposes Egyptian participation in the Sudan ceased to exist. The Egyptian army had been sent home to Cairo. It was followed by a stream of lesser Egyptian officials, clerks, technicians, and teachers. Sudanese filled some of their places, Lebanese staffed others, but the rest remained empty, and the modernization of the Sudan was consequently constricted.

The Sudanese revolt of 1924 was not as important as the reaction to it. The discontent in the Sudan had been limited to a tiny minority, largely subverted by Egyptians. The overwhelming number of Sudanese tribesmen and leaders alike remained steadfastly loyal to their British rulers. The British repaid this devotion with confidence, but they viewed with alarm the new class of educated Sudanese they had created. Ironically, just as Wingate had sought to protect the Sudan against a rising of the tribes, his successors now sought to check the Sudanese elite, whose liberalism could not be reconciled with the authoritarianism of imperial rule. The military school was closed. Courses designed to train junior administrators were abandoned, and Gordon College and its products were regarded with suspicion if not contempt. Greater reliance was placed upon converting the tribal authorities into agents of the administration rather than handing administrative duties to Western-educated Sudanese civil servants. Such a policy not only helped to remedy the loss of Egyptian officials, but it coincided with the colonial policy of indirect rule which was then being hailed as the key to the stable advancement of dependent peoples. Indeed, the whole trend of British policy in the Sudan until the Second World War was to isolate the Sudanese elite, who were watched, suspected, and even feared. Governor-General Sir John Maffey succinctly betrayed this attitude when he wrote in 1927:

The granting of powers to native magistrates and sheikhs is more in keeping with the prime principle [devolution of authority to tribal chiefs], but here again unless such machinery stands on a true native and traditional basis it is off the main drive. Advisory Councils cropped up as a possible means to our end but the proposal was not well received and I think there were good grounds for hesitation. Later on in certain intelligentsia areas, when we have made the Sudan safe for autocracy, such Councils may be innocuous or even desirable. Also Advisory Councils to Chiefs would be in keeping with the broad principle. Otherwise Advisory Councils contain the seeds of grave danger and eventually present a free platform for capture by a pushful intelligentsia.

If the encouragement of native authority in the true sense of the Milner formula is our accepted policy, before old traditions die we ought to get on with the extension and expansion in every direction, thereby sterilizing and localising the political germs which must spread from the lower Nile into Khartoum.

Under the impulse of new ideas and with the rise of a new generation, old traditions may pass away with astonishing rapidity. It is advisable to fortify them while the memories of Mahdism and Omdurman are still vivid and while tribal sanctions are still a living force. The death of two or three veterans in a tribe may constitute a serious break with the past.

Such anxiety on my part may seem far-fetched to those who know the out-lying parts of the Sudan. Perhaps it is, for I realize the wide range of differing conditions. But I have watched an old generation give place to a new one in India and I have seen how easily vague political unrest swept over even backward peoples simply because we had allowed the old forms to crumble away. Yet the native states in India remain safe and secure in the hands of hereditary rulers, loyal to the King Emperor, showing what we might have done if we had followed a different course. We failed to put up a shield between the agitator and the bureaucracy.

Political considerations are still easy in the Sudan. But nothing stands still and in Khartoum we are already in touch with the outposts of new political forces. For a long time the British Administrative Officer in the Sudan has functioned as "Father of the People." In many places he will for a long time so continue. But this cannot last. The bureaucracy must yield either to an autocratic or to a democratic movement and the dice are loaded in favour of the latter. If we desire the former, the British Officer must realize that it is his duty to lay down the role of Father of the People. He must entrust it to the natural leaders of the people whom he must support and influence as occasion requires. In that manner the country will be parcelled out into nicely balanced compartments, protective glands against the septic germs which will inevitably be passed on from the Khartoum of the future.

Failing this armour we shall be involved in a losing fight throughout the length and breadth of the land. . . .[6]

[6] "Minute by his Excellency the Governor General" (Sir John Maffey), January 1, 1927, Sudan Government Archives, Civil Secretary's Archives, I/9/33.

FIVE

NASSER'S EGYPT AND THE INDEPENDENT

SUDAN

Nasser's Egypt

By 1952 the general disorganization of Egyptian political and economic life had reached a crisis. Political violence was endemic. The parliamentary system had ceased to work. Egypt's relationship with Great Britain was totally unresolved. Indeed, the failure of Great Britain and Egypt to negotiate a new treaty after the war served to initiate new outbursts of political violence. The issues that divided Britain and Egypt were the old ones, jurisdiction over the Sudan and the garrisoning of British troops in the Suez Canal zone. In 1951 the Wafd, in a bold bid to recapture popularity, proclaimed the abolition of the treaty of 1936. This step led inevitably to an intensification of violence against British troops in the canal base. Guerrilla attacks were launched against the British army. Egyptian workers began a boycott against the base which was extraordinarily effective, and more than any other single factor brought home to the British the ineffectiveness of the base without some measure of Egyptian support. The guerrilla attacks were also irritating, and eventually British troops retaliated against their antagonists. Unfortunately, the Wafd had done almost nothing to prepare the country for the outbreak of violence. They unscrupulously sought political power without reference to the consequences in human suffering. In January 1952 British troops overpowered a unit of auxiliary Egyptian police in Ismailia. The news of the event circulated among the people of Cairo, whose frenzy and hatred found expression in mob action. On January 26, 1952, with the Wafdist government unable to offer either leadership or protection, the famous burning of Cairo began.

Early on that morning mobs of students began to congregate across the Nile outside the center of the city. The government was appraised of the situation but was too fearful of incurring unpopularity to curtail the mob. The students, swelled by many other elements and certainly by most political agitators in Cairo, were permitted to cross over the Nile and enter the center of the city. The uncontrolled mob began to set fire to buildings. The special targets of their hatred were buildings which symbolized the West and the influence of Western civilization—cinemas, European hotels, sporting clubs, restaurants. The mob prevented the fire brigade from putting out the fires and was too large for the police to control. For the better part of the day there was complete anarchy in the center of Cairo. Egypt's most luxurious hotel, the Shepheard's, was burnt to the ground. An exclusive British sporting club suffered the same fate. Finally, and only late in the afternoon, the army was called in to quell the rioting.

The burning of Cairo demonstrated the inability of the Wafd to provide leadership in those troubled times. The Wafdist ministry resigned and was replaced by a series of interim governments whose leaders were not drawn from the major political parties. The ministries were headed by men who were civil servants rather than politicians. Some efforts were made to restore order and economic vitality, but the forces of opposition were still too strong and reforms were blocked. In any case, civilian government had only a short lease on life. Younger discontented elements in the army were planning a *coup d'état*. On July 23, 1952, just six months after the burning of Cairo, a segment of the army seized power.

A great deal has been written about military rule in Egypt, much of which invariably can be classified under one of three categories: that the army was the only organized element in a totally disrupted society, thus its acquisition of power; that the discontented officers had long been planning for the overthrow of civilian government; and finally, that the army had clear-cut ideas for the transformation of Egyptian society.

The emphasis upon the army as the only organized element in Egypt overlooks the crucial fact that the army was itself deeply divided. Nearly all of the older and senior officers were men of the old regime, mostly appointees of the Egyptian monarchy and deeply involved in the maintenance of the existing order. King Faruq (1936-52), was not so naïve as to allow elements hostile to himself to attain top positions within the army. The opposition within the army came from the younger and junior officers, the so-called Free Officers group. Their *coup d'état* had to be effected not only against the king and the politicians but also against conservative elements in the army. Division within the army came to the surface in 1951, when the Free Officers ran their own candidate for president of the officers club and defeated the nominee of the king. But even within the Free Officers movement there were deep divisions. All were disillusioned with the existing state of affairs, but there were left and right wings within the movement. Some of the officers had attachments to the Muslim Brotherhood, while others were sympathetic to communism. In reality, the reason that the army, although divided, was not paralyzed like other organizations in Egypt was the shrewd leadership of Colonel Nasser. The strength of his personality alone held together the various factions of the Free Officers, and he was extraordinarily adept at keeping his intentions a secret from opponents in the army.

Accepting information provided by members of the Free Officers themselves, many writers on contemporary Egypt have argued that the Free Officers organization had come into existence long before the *coup d'état* of 1952. To be sure, many of the leaders of the movement were late-1930s graduates of the military college. Many had been classmates. In their official posts they enjoyed opportunities to meet together and discuss Egyptian affairs. Very early in their careers they expressed dissatisfaction with the old order. The 1942 crisis and the humiliation of the army in the 1948 Palestinian campaign quickened their discontent, but it was not until 1949 that a formal organization came into existence. Although they believed that the old order must be supplanted, at this time they did not see themselves as the instrument of change. The Free Officers organization was set up, in part, to protect the younger and more radical men in the army against the intrigues of the king. In part, it was also established to debate and circulate the ideas of the young officers more widely throughout the army. It had both a civilian and a military wing for popularizing its ideas, although the civilian wing soon fell into disuse. Only the extraordinary breakdown in political and economic order in 1951 and 1952 convinced the Free Officers that the army must play a predominant role in the politics of Egypt.

Thus, in July 1952 the army carried out its *coup d'état*. It was not meant to be a full-scale revolution. The revolutionary aspect came later in piecemeal fashion as the army leaders were confronted with unexpected and specific problems. Moreover, the Free Officers held a variety of opinions. Some, influenced by communist ideology, favored radical social and economic reforms. Others wanted to implement some of the ideas of the Muslim Brotherhood, making Egypt into an Islamic state and purging it of many secular and Western elements. The majority of the leaders, including Colonel Nasser, seem to have regarded it as their task to purge Egypt of its corruption and return the country to civilian and parliamentary government. It was only after difficulties were encountered in achieving these limited goals that more radical policies began to be devised. Nevertheless, even these later policies did not derive from a clear-cut set of principles. They were improvised under the pressure of events. And even to this day the Nasser regime has not been doctrinaire; it is still characterized by flexibility and improvisation.

One goal the military sought to realize was the deposition of King Faruq. The king symbolized the old order, corrupt, dissolute, selfish and pleasure-loving, with no feeling for the country and its people. He stood convicted in their minds for undermining the war effort in Palestine and even benefiting from this action. He and his family were the largest landholders in Egypt. The military carried out the deposition with great skill for it was no easy matter with British troops poised in the Suez Canal zone. On the morning of the takeover the army broadcast news of its seizure of power and exhorted the populace to remain calm. Likewise, they promised that their seizure of power was purely an internal matter and brought no threat to any foreign interest in Egypt. This last, of course, was designed for foreign consumption, especially the British. Very little else was said in these early broadcasts, and nothing about the position of the king. Three days later, after no foreign intervention had occurred and stability was assured, the king was ordered to abdicate. Since he was unable to rally any support, Faruq had no alternative and left Egypt. The fiction of monarchy was maintained for a while longer. A regency was appointed for Faruq's son and heir to the throne, but in a short while this institution was abolished, and Egypt declared a republic.

The younger officers, of course, had other goals when they seized power. In their discussions and especially in their secret pamphlets they had criticized corruption in the old regime, the reactionary landholders, the lack of vitality in the political parties, and the need for accelerated economic growth. Through his reading as a young man

Nasser had been attracted to extremist nationalism and reformed Islam. In secondary school he had read the biography of Mustafa Kamil, collections of articles from *al-Liwa*, the newspaper of the National Party, and many of the works of Egyptian Muslim intellectuals (Muhammad Abduh, Ahmad Amin, and Tawfiq al-Hakim). At the military school he had read biographies of Bonaparte, Ataturk, Bismarck, Churchill, and Gordon, and the multivolumed political history of Egypt written by Abd al-Rahman al-Rafii, an ardent apostle of Egypt's National Party. Of the twenty-three directing officers of the military *coup d'état*, only three were European-educated. Most were drawn from the lower echelons of the so-called salaried middle class, sons of postal clerks and government bureaucrats who had entered the military college in the 1930s when it was first thrown open to all classes of Egyptian society. On the whole, these men were suspicious of rationalist liberalism and democracy. Their ideas were vague and ill-defined, and it was more the pressure of events than ideology which crystallized the thinking of the new military regime. In particular, two crucial events during the first few months shaped the attitudes of the new leaders: the workers' strike and riot at Kafr al-Dawar textile mills, and the passage of the agrarian reform law.

In August 1952, just one month after the *coup d'état*, workers at the important textile center of Kafr al-Dawar struck and rioted. These serious disturbances were eventually quelled by units of the police and army. The military regime brutally crushed the rioters. Leaders of the workers' faction were brought to trial and given heavy sentences. During the trials the military regime tried to make it appear that the textile workers were among the most favored groups in Egypt and that the rioting had actually been engineered by opponents of the new regime, presumably by landlords and old regime politicians, to embarrass and subvert the government. What seems a more reasonable explanation is that the seizure of power by the military on July 23 had aroused elements of Egyptian society to the prospects of change. One of the best organized of the lower class elements had then struck to dramatize its position. The severe reprisals taken by the government clearly indicated that, at least at this stage, the regime had little intention of turning the *coup d'état* into a full-scale social revolution. Their repression of the workers was also a demonstration of support for the industrialists and capitalists in Egypt.

The second important development was the agrarian reform scheme of September 1952. Land reform was clearly one of the goals of all progressive and reformist elements in Egypt, and not surprisingly some sort of land redistribution scheme followed closely on the heels of the *coup*. The type of land reform enacted is, however, quite revealing of the social and political leanings of the new leaders. The scheme was a moderate one. The reactionary landlords, supported by politicians of the old order, of course wanted no real land redistribution. The Muslim Brotherhood wanted a very conservative program, fixing the maximum limits of an individual's land at five hundred feddans, a very sizable holding indeed. More radical elements favored reducing private holdings to fifty or one hundred feddans and giving minimal compensation to the expropriated holders. The regime finally decided to fix two hundred feddans as the maximum holding for any one person and allowed one hundred additional feddans to a family. Land taken in excess of this figure was to be compensated through state bonds and then to be distributed among the small peasantry. All of the land belonging to the king and his family was expropriated without compensation and added to the general fund for redistribution. Although the land reform gave land to peasants, it did not provide much land for the already large landless peasant class. In fact, those provisions in the law for the protection of the rural proletariat were not generally enforced. Moreover, estates of two or three hundred feddans are quite large in a country where yields per acre are so extraordinarily high. Thus, only the truly large landholders were hard hit by the law. The government itself retained a large portion of the expropriated land and became the largest landowner in Egypt.

During the land redistribution the military regime learned important new lessons. They realized fully the very considerable opposition to this type of reform among the parties of the old regime. After their seizure of power the young officers had appointed Ali Mahir as prime minister. He was generally recognized as a progressive and uncorruptible political figure, even though a representative of the prerevolutionary era. Other men of similar reputation were incorporated into his ministry. Nevertheless, Ali Mahir balked at enacting the land reform scheme propounded by the young officers and resigned in September 1952. The rather general opposition to land reform among the older politicians disillusioned the military revolutionaries from seeking further points of agreement with political representatives of the pre-1952 era.

The military leaders had exhorted Egypt's traditional parties to purge themselves of reactionary and corrupt elements as a prelude to the restoration of parliamentary government. There was considerable reluctance in the parties to effect such changes. Indeed, whether the military ever would have considered conditions ripe for a return to a parliamentary regime is a debatable issue, but unquestionably the unwillingness of the parties to cooperate left Nasser little choice in this matter. For example, the Wafd kept its old leader, Nahas, as honorary president, while another party declared that it would make no changes because it had no errors to correct. It is hardly surprising, then, that the military gradually assumed direct control of all the ministries. In February 1953 political parties were dissolved, the only exception being the still favored Muslim Brotherhood.

Certainly one of the fundamental goals of the government was to accelerate the modernization of Egypt. Economic disorder had prevailed since 1945. In reality, agrarian reform and the suppression of rioters at Kafr al-Dawar were an integral part of the economic goals of the new regime. Agrarian reform had multiple aims. It was intended to destroy the economic and political power of the landholding aristocracy and to redistribute wealth among the peasants. It was also designed to stimulate economic growth. The new government hoped that land redistributed among the peasants would be more intensively cultivated and would give higher yields. Even more important was the expectation that capital formerly expended upon the purchase of surplus agricultural land would now be redirected into the industrial sphere. These supplies of capital would thus accelerate industrialization, on which the government pinned its hopes for economic growth and a rise in standards of living. In fact, the military was turning to Egypt's industrial and financial class at this stage as the chief instrument of industrial growth, regarding its own role essentially as that of providing favorable conditions in which this class could work. Efforts were also made to attract foreign capital to Egypt. The government permitted foreign capitalists to hold 51 per cent of the shares of joint-stock companies instead of the previous 49 per cent. An independent German firm was given a contract for the establishment of an iron and steel plant at Helwan near Cairo. The state thus was giving private capital, both foreign and Egyptian, a large role in the new order. It is in this light that the severe reaction to the worker's riot at Kafr al-Dawar must be seen, for the military regime wanted to disassociate itself from close identification with Egypt's proletariat.

In only rather limited ways, then, was the military regime in its first year a revolution. The king had been deposed, political parties dissolved, and Egypt proclaimed a republic. The political power of the old aristocracy had been undermined, especially by the diminution of its economic power through land reform. But in other areas the new regime had moved cautiously. Economic and social reform had been limited to land redistribution. The private and even the foreign sectors of the economy remained largely undisturbed.

The increasing radicalization of Egyptian policy which was to mark the next decade (1954-64) resulted from an interaction of domestic and foreign pressures. Once again the empirical attitude of the Egyptian leaders, their flexibility in most but not all cases, and their capacity to improvise were paramount. Although domestic and foreign policy were inextricably intermeshed, certain periods were clearly dominated by foreign policy issues, others by domestic considerations. In each sphere, however, Egyptian policy moved toward more radical positions.

Following the consolidation of the *coup*, the new regime naturally turned to the question of Egypt's relationship with Great Britain. This was, of course, a crucial matter, for the events leading up to the *coup* of July 1952 had been initiated by hostilities between the Egyptian people and British troops. So long as this relationship was not resolved, there was the threat of violence at home and possible British military intervention from abroad. Once they had consolidated their power in Egypt the military was dealing from a position of strength in their negotiations with the British. Consequently, they did not have to use foreign relations to whip up support for their regime, as the Wafd had done. They were also willing to make concessions which other politicians would have feared to grant. By the treaty of 1954 Egypt and Great Britain agreed upon the evacuation of British troops from the Suez Canal base, to be reoccupied only if an Arab state or Turkey were invaded. The government also agreed that the Sudanese people should be given the right to settle their own fate by means of an election. To the extremists in Egypt the treaty was too compromising, especially by opening the door to eventual Sudanese independence, but it demonstrated the realism of Egypt's new leaders. The withdrawal of British troops removed the principal cause of discontent and permitted the Egyptian government to concentrate on domestic reforms and to indulge in an independent foreign policy. Although it flew in the face of all previous nationalist demands, the concession on the Sudan was the only realistic position to assume. Great Britain would have accepted nothing less, nor would Egypt have been able to govern the Sudan without British consent.

The treaty negotiations of 1954 brought to the surface the internal sources of opposition to the regime, and during the spring of that year domestic tensions once again dominated the scene. The military was still far from unified. Although the seizure of power had been engineered by Nasser and other young officers, General Naguib had been closely associated with the new government and was at first its spokesman. Naguib was an older man, a senior officer, who nevertheless held progressive ideas and was quite willing to cooperate with the young officers. Nasser had kept himself very much in the background, and Naguib, a kindly and tolerant man, had won acclaim from the Egyptian people. Other groups still had considerable power. The Muslim Brotherhood had been permitted to remain even after the dissolution of political parties. Communist and socialist sympathizers were widespread among Egypt's student population. Politicians of the old order stood on the sidelines awaiting any faltering in the new regime. A rift began to grow between Nasser and Naguib, partly over power, partly over policies. Naguib was aware of his growing popularity and wanted to increase his power. He was also more favorably disposed toward the reintroduction of parliamentary government than was Nasser. In February 1954 the ruling organ of the military, the Revolutionary Command Council (R.C.C.) announced the resignation of Naguib. This announcement created great resentment in Egypt and unified the opposition. Left-wing elements and politicians of the old regime were anxious for a return of parliamentary government. The Muslim Brotherhood did not favor parliamentary government but saw an opportunity to overthrow the R.C.C. The intensity of opposition obviously surprised Nasser, and the R.C.C. was forced to make concessions. Naguib was reinstated with extended powers, and the R.C.C. even announced the imminent dissolution of military rule and the reestablishment of democratic government.

Nasser was only biding his time for a more favorable opportunity to strike again at his opponents. This time he worked more carefully behind the scenes, isolated his antagonists, and cut them down one by one. The first to go was Naguib. Nasser had undermined Naguib's support in the army, and he was able to dismiss Naguib from his positions and put him under house arrest. The decree for the end of military rule was suspended. A Muslim Brother's attempt to assassinate Nasser in October 1954 served as the pretext for attacking the Muslim Brotherhood. The Brotherhood was dissolved, and its leaders were thrown into jail. Many of these Muslim Brothers were later brought to trial and given severe sentences. Nasser now came forward as the unchallenged leader of the new government, having purged his own ranks of opposition and having struck at other sources of power in Egypt. The power of the Muslim Brotherhood was broken, although recent trials in connection with another attempt in 1965 to assassinate Nasser indicate a new growth of Muslim Brotherhood power today. Nevertheless, Nasser's preeminent position in the Egyptian hierarchy of power has not been seriously threatened since 1954.

The drive and energy of the regime was next felt once again in Egypt's external relations. Actually, the events of 1955 and 1956 resulting in the formulation of Egypt's foreign policy of neutrality and the nationalization of the Suez Canal Company were partly forced on the Egyptian government by attitudes and policies of foreign governments. A crucial factor in turning Egypt's attention to foreign affairs was a series of Israeli raids across the Egyptian border. These were costly to the Egyptian army, and they also impressed Nasser with the need to strengthen the Egyptian army. Undoubtedly, the Egyptian government would sooner or later have sought to develop its military potential, in spite of the raids, but certainly the troubled relations between Israel and Egypt contributed to militarism in Egypt.

Although Nasser would not become a member of any Western defensive alliance, he still tended to look to the West for military support during this stage of the Egyptian revolution from 1954 to 1955. No overt moves had been made in the direction of the communist world. The Western powers regarded the Middle East as its own sphere of influence, and Nasser's quiescent behavior did not represent a challenge to the West. The Baghdad Pact, the Bandung conference, and Egypt's inability to obtain from the United States what it regarded as an adequate supply of arms for its defense soon altered Nasser's attitude.

The creation of the Baghdad Pact in 1955 was a bitter pill for the Egyptian government. Even before the *coup* of July 1952 the Egyptian government had refused to join a Western defensive alliance in the Middle East. Indeed, the British had tried to substitute a combined Western and Egyptian military command of the Suez Canal base in place of its own control, but nationalist sentiment in Egypt was too strong even to compromise on a joint command. The creation of the Baghdad Pact, which included Turkey, Iraq, Iran, Pakistan, and Great Britain and was supported by the United States, alarmed Egypt. Although the alliance was originally designed as a northern tier of non-Arab states, the inclusion of Iraq, an Arab state and a member of the Arab League receiving large arms shipments from the United States, appeared ominous to the Egyptians. Nasser did not share the Western view that the Middle East was a power vacuum which would be an easy prey to communism without some form of Western military support. Rather, he felt that the Baghdad Pact was a device for perpetuating Western political and economic controls over the area to keep it weak and unable to solve its own problems, and thus to retain its dependence on the West. Moreover, he feared that the Baghdad Pact might be used to threaten the Egyptian revolution. Iraq, the only Arab member, was the very antithesis of Egypt. Monarchist, run by landlords and traditional politicians with conservative economic and social policies, Iraq might serve as a rallying force in the Arab East for conservative forces that felt threatened by the achievements of the Egyptian revolution. Consequently, Nasser turned the full force of his propaganda against the Baghdad Pact and, of course, against its creators, the Western powers.

In April 1955 Nasser represented Egypt at the Afro-Asian conference in Bandung. His contacts there with Asian nationalist leaders, particularly Nehru, immensely stimulated his thinking on neutralism. Communist China was very ably represented at the conference by Chou en-Lai, and it was shortly after his return from Bandung that the Egyptian government recognized Communist China. Still, in 1955 when Nasser was seeking arms to strengthen his military position, he turned to the West. The Americans were reluctant to meet all of his demands. If the delicate balance of arms between Israel and the Arab states was upset, they feared an arms race in the Middle East. Nasser was dismayed, for he felt his army did not have the proper equipment to defend itself against Israeli incursions into Egyptian territory. Yet he pressed on with his negotiations with the United States, and only when rebuffed did he turn to the Soviet bloc. In September 1955 Egypt signed an arms agreement with Czechoslovakia, by which the Czechs undertook to supply the needed arms to Egypt without conditions. This was a major communist breakthrough in the Middle East, ending Western control over the supply of arms. It demonstrated to other countries in the Middle East and elsewhere that they could obtain arms from rival sources without compromising their independence.

These very disturbing events were but a prelude, however, to an even bigger crisis, the nationalization of the Suez Canal Company. Egypt had been negotiating with the Western powers to finance the new High Dam at Aswan. An agreement had tentatively been reached in which the United States, Britain, and the World Bank were to provide the necessary capital. The details, however, had not been completed, and when negotiations over them stalled, Secretary of State John Foster Dulles decided to withdraw American financing for the project. Although Dulles argued that American support was being withdrawn because of weaknesses in the Egyptian economy, he appeared more intent on punishing and embarrassing the Egyptian government for its flirtation with the Soviet bloc. Nasser countered with an even bolder move. Speaking to a crowd in Alexandria in July 1956, he launched into a long harangue against Western imperalism. The special object of his attack was the Suez Canal, which, he charged, had been built with Egyptian labor and capital and from which Egypt had received virtually no benefit. Near the climax of his speech he quoted the profits of the Suez Canal Company; these, he said, would go a long way toward financing Egypt's Aswan Dam. He then dramatically announced his decision to nationalize the Suez Canal Company. Fair compensation was to be paid its stockholders, but its profits henceforth were to go to the Egyptian government.

Nasser's bold stroke nearly brought about his own downfall. But the Anglo-French invasion and the Israeli attack, although militarily victorious, were diplomatic failures, and thus insured the independence of Egypt and turned Nasser into an Egyptian and Middle Eastern hero. The new regime had succeeded in asserting its control over one of the most valuable waterways in the world, and it had done this in defiance of two of the greatest Western powers, once colonial masters of the Middle East.

Although the nationalization of the canal may have appeared an angry and hasty response to Dulles' withdrawal of funds for the Aswan Dam, this was surely not the case. Most Egyptian ministers did not know of the plan until an hour before Nasser made his speech, but the Egyptian government had been discussing nationalization of the Suez Canal long before July 1956, and it is doubtful if the canal would have remained an international company until its concession was due to expire in 1968. The state of Egyptian preparedness for nationalization can perhaps be most clearly assessed by the efficient operation of the canal after nationalization. This difficult task was carried out with great skill under Mahmud Yunis.

The international dispute of 1955-56, which culminated in the Anglo-French-Israeli invasion of Egypt, paved the way for the "Egyptianization" of many British and French companies. Banks, insurance firms, and other economic enterprises were sequestrated, and their assets were sold to private Egyptian firms. It was, in fact, in this period that Egyptian state-supported capitalism attained its greatest preeminence. Following the *coup* of July 1952 the new regime had attempted to encourage both Egyptian and foreign capital. With the Egyptianization of British and French companies foreign capital was pushed aside in favor of private Egyptian capital. Between 1956 and 1960 an alliance was struck between the military government and the great Egyptian finance and industrial capitalists, the close ties with the Soviet bloc notwithstanding. Egyptian capitalism was still tightly concentrated and monopolistic. Two large groups controlled nearly all the large-scale economic enterprises, the Misr group and the enterprises of Ahmad Abbud. The close relationship between state and private capital must certainly be remembered when assessing the radical aspect of the military government. Although the state was simultaneously enlarging its powers as overseer and regulator of the economy, it still pinned its hopes for Egyptian industrialization on its alliance with Egyptian capitalism.

The alliance was further strengthened by the union of Syria and Egypt in 1958. The capitalists in particular were eager for this new field of economic enterprise, and they looked upon the union as a means for facilitating the flow of Egyptian capital into Syria. Actually, the union was not brought about primarily for economic reasons but because of chaotic political conditions in Syria. Syrian communist elements were very strong, and in 1957-58 there were serious disturbances in the country. These alarmed the United States and Turkey. The American Mediterranean fleet sailed into the eastern Mediterranean, and Turkish troops were moved to the Turkish-Syrian border. Under pressure of these threats Syrian politicians turned to President Nasser, seeking his agreement for a union of the two countries. Nasser was reluctant. Although a keen exponent of Arab unity, he did not think the time was ripe for union. In his view they were at different stages of development. Egypt had executed a revolution against its landholding aristocracy. The country was governed by a military regime. But Syria still had large landholders and a more open and competitive political system. Yet Nasser accepted a union principally because he feared that political disturbances in Syria might lead to an increase of foreign influences in the Arab world.

The union with Syria and the alliance with Egyptian capitalism were short-lived. There were simply too many areas of conflict with the Nasser government. The great stumbling block was the inability of private capital to attain the rate of industrialization set by the state. The government became increasingly convinced that finance and industrial capitalism was not the answer to Egypt's need for industrialization and decided to assume this role itself. The first move, which one author has described as "the dismantling of the bourgeoisie," took place in February 1960. Egypt's two great banks, The National Bank of Egypt and Misr Bank, were nationalized. There was nothing radical in the nationalization of the National Bank, for it was a bank of issue, and the government was able to argue that the state should control the institution through which currency was distributed. The Misr Bank, on the other hand, was the central financial institution of the Misr group, which had a hand in nearly all the major financial and industrial enterprises in Egypt. Its nationalization dealt a severe blow to private capitalism. These steps were followed in June and July 1961 by a host of social legislation by which a very large segment of the Egyptian economy was brought under direct state regulation. The companies affected were divided into three categories. Those in the first category, including banks, insurance companies, and fifty other firms, were nationalized outright. Those in the second category, eighty-three companies in light industry, turned over at least 50 per cent of their capital to the state, while 145 independent companies in the third group were permitted a more limited obligation to the state. According to a law of December 1961, all existing companies (367 in total) were to be organized into thirty-eight public corporations administered by state technocrats. At the same time the state carried its agrarian reform one step further, reducing the maximum size of individual owner-ship from two to one hundred feddans. Thus the state became the leader and supervisor of the industrialization of Egypt. Nevertheless, the private sector remains, including some heavy industry, larger amounts of middle and light industry, one quarter of the external commerce, three quarters of internal commerce, most of the land, and most immobile property.

One of the casualties of this spate of radical social legislation was the union with Syria. The new laws increased the tension between the centralized military regime in Egypt and the more free-enterprise-minded Syrians. Syrian politicians had chafed under Nasser's domi-nation of the union. When the Egyptians tried to apply these laws to Syria, large segments of the Syrian population became alienated, and in September 1961 Syria revolted. The Egyptian leaders were expelled, and Syria declared itself independent of Egypt.

Most commentators have referred to the last decade and a half in Egypt as the Egyptian revolution. Yet in many respects this pe-riod has not possessed characteristics commonly associated with other revolutions. The leaders, when they came to power, did not have the ideological fervor of the Russian or French revolutionaries. They had some basic goals: to rid the country of foreign occupation and to undercut the economic and political power of the old land-holding aristocracy, but beyond these general ends they did not have any concrete plans. Nearly all close observers have noted the ideolog-ical poverty of the new leaders. These were military men, not in-tellectuals. Moreover, throughout their period of rule, these leaders displayed a flexibility, an ability to change direction uncommon in the first generation of revolutionaries. Perhaps the one great excep-tion was the breakup of the union of Syria and Egypt; here President Nasser seems to have applied decrees derived from Egyptian experi-ence without reference to differing conditions in Syria. The military regime was very quickly able to jettison its own doctrinaire right and left wings.

This lack of ideological and doctrinaire fervor has prompted a few people to suggest that the Nasser government was not revolutionary at all. Indeed, one Egyptian leftist has argued that the Nasser government prevented a real left-wing revolution in 1952.[1] By forcing their way to power in 1952 and then carrying out moderate land reforms, the military forestalled a union of peasants, workers, and intellectuals and a real socialist revolution. This view certainly cannot be idly dismissed. The willingness of the military to work with Egyptian capitalism until this alliance proved itself a failure indicates an essential conservatism in the regime. Whether the lower class element, the peasantry and urban proletariat, would have been able to bring about a revolution appears dubious, but it is certainly significant that the army did intercede before other, more radical elements had a chance to capture the leadership of the revolution. While the military were often propelled by events beyond their control, at no time did they constitute the most radical element in Egypt.

These facts should not obscure the truly revolutionary aspects of the military regime. Its impact throughout the Middle East and in the rest of the non-Western world has been impressive. If, in fact, one looks at the reactions to the Nasser regime throughout the rest of the world, one can see more clearly its most revolutionary aspects. The regime has been praised or censored mainly for its nationalism, its neutralism, and its socialist tendencies. In the Western world its nationalization of foreign assets has caused great discontent. Its pursuit of a neutralist foreign policy has also been resented, although in recent years the Western world has come to accept this policy. Throughout the Middle East the socialistic land reforming programs of the regime have captured almost as much attention as Egypt's defiance of the West. What Nasser would regard as regimes of the old order have especially felt threatened by his appeal to the younger generation. Nasser has been, in fact, the first Arab leader to achieve a socialist and nationalist program. His example has been immensely stimulating to other leaders.

Nationalism and socialism have been the two foundations of the Egyptian revolution. Democracy, of course, has not. In many ways Egypt has behaved like other revolutionary countries in attempting to safeguard and even extend its revolution. The French and Russian revolutionaries tried to eradicate opponents of their revolutions, both to protect the revolution at home from its enemies and to extend the revolution into other areas. Egypt's leaders have similarly sought

[1] Anouar Abdel-Malek, *Egypte: Société Militaire* (Paris: 1962).

to undercut all those domestic elements considered inimical to the regime. They have attempted to win the same kind of commitment to the government and widespread acceptance of its goals as did the French and Russian revolutionaries but, of course, without their success. The Egyptians have feared counterrevolution from the more conservative regimes of the Arab East, with the support of the Western powers, and in a more positive fashion they have also sought to extend their own revolutionary principles of nationalism and socialism throughout the Arab world. This interpretation does not deny the nonrevolutionary, purely imperialistic aspects of Egyptian involvement in the affairs of the Middle East. It only suggests that part of this involvement stems from the spirit of the revolution itself.

The new regime has reinforced certain recurrent traits of Egyptian history. A centralized government and military rule have again come to dominate political affairs in Egypt. Ever since Egyptians began to control the flow of the Nile for irrigation and cultivation, the central government has assumed great importance. The Mamluks certainly brought military government to Egypt, and under Muhammad Ali the military was the focus for Egyptian modernization. Nevertheless, Egypt in the 1960s is undoubtedly more unlike Egypt in the 1750s than like it. One of the major differences is the breakdown in local self-sufficiency and the resulting increase of the power of the central government. To be sure, a centralized government has long existed, but its role was hitherto generally limited to tax collection, the operation of the irrigation system, and the maintenance of a minimum of public security. Local bodies, particularly kinship and village organizations, retained considerable autonomy from the central government.

Modernization has broadened the functions and powers of the central government. The Nasser regime has accelerated this tendency, increasing the amount and diversity of governmental activity. The government's control over the economy is but one illustration of this development. Whereas before 1800 the state controlled the economy largely through taxation, under the new regime the state itself has become one of the most active economic agencies in the country. The modern Egyptian government disposes of many times more of the gross national product than its predecessors did.

The new military government also presents some striking contrasts with the old. Most obvious is the composition of the present military leadership, which is drawn from the Egyptian populace and not an alien oligarchy. Nasser and his colleagues, in fact, came from a lower stratum of society than the leaders they supplanted, and consequently, have a more sympathetic attitude toward the lower classes of Egypt. In general, the army has been an instrument of the new salaried, educated middle class. Moreover, while traditional Egyptian military oligarchies have been concerned with maximizing only their own wealth, the new government has clearly sought to modernize Egypt generally and to raise the standards of living of all. Thus, the traditional gap between the rulers and the ruled in Egypt has been broken down, though perhaps only a little.

The Nasser regime has promised and worked for all these achievements: economic development, rising standards of living, education for all, and political integration between the rulers and the ruled. While the government has been pragmatic throughout, its improvisations have always been oriented toward these goals. How well has the regime realized its aims? Despite its own resolve, the objectives have continued to elude the government. Economic development has been the motive force for many of the significant changes in state policy under Nasser, and there have been impressive achievements, particularly the Aswan Dam. Industry, with immense government support, is the fastest growing sector of the economy. Nevertheless, most industries are still not competitive on the world market, and they exist only because of state support. The per capita national income has not risen greatly under Nasser. There are recent reports of considerable food shortages. Egypt's balance of payments problem has grown serious, and the government has exhausted its foreign currency in its efforts to stimulate economic growth and carry on an expensive foreign policy. Most revealing, one must not forget that one of every two Egyptians is fed by the grain surplus of the United States through the Food for Peace program.

Education was to be a handmaid of economic development and political integration. It was to provide trained manpower for economic growth and a means for mobilizing the population for action toward economic and political goals. In the last decade school enrollments have increased to four million. University education has been expanded. In 1961, 16.5 per cent of the state budget was expended on education. Moreover, important modifications have been made in the traditional dual educational system. Until 1949 Egypt had two sets of schools: primary, secondary, and higher schools for the wealthy, and elementary schools for the masses. There was hardly any access from the elementary schools into the other system. In 1949 an attempt was made to improve the training in the elementary schools. Then in 1956 the first stage of schooling was unified and made coeducational. Despite these achievements, Egypt's educational system remains incomplete. The over-all illiteracy rate was 72 per cent in 1957, 60 per cent for men and 84 per cent for women. The quality of education has not kept pace with the quantity. Students appear to lack the initiative of their Western counterparts, preferring to enter safe positions in the government bureaucracy rather than striking out on careers in commerce and industry. The vast expansion of education has had to be geared to an equally fast-growing population. This has been possible in many areas, but at all times there have been problems of employing well qualified staff.

Various attempts to associate the population more closely with the government through the introduction of responsible and representative political institutions have not been very successful. The most recent effort was the 1960 reorganization of local government and the creation of the Arab Socialist Union. The population, however, has remained skeptical, and the government has been reluctant to give popularly selected organizations any real power.

Undoubtedly, population growth has been the single most important obstacle to Egyptian modernization, nullifying many of the economic and educational gains. The Nasser government's heavy expenditure on armaments and its involvement in expensive military campaigns in Yemen have not helped to correct these domestic problems and in fact have hindered economic development and exhausted Egypt's foreign exchange. Increasingly, the Nasser government is finding it difficult to be simultaneously successful on both the foreign and domestic fronts, creating frustrations at home, impatience abroad, and the climate of discontent that encourages the radicals of improvisation and dismays the rationalists of planned modernization.

The Independent Sudan

Before the outbreak of the Second World War a profound change came over the Sudan government and was reflected in the new spirit with which the British officials approached the task of governing the Sudan. New men came out from Britain, recruited in the same manner as their predecessors and from the same institutions, but with a remarkably different attitude. Born in time of war, reared in the unsettled decade which followed, and educated in the Depression, these young administrators were in many ways better trained in administrative techniques but possessed little of the olympian confidence which had enabled their Victorian forerunners to extend British control to the farthest reaches of a vast and inhospitable land. These new men were no longer convinced that Great Britain held a divinely appointed monopoly on the art of governing and for the first time questioned by what right, other than conquest, the British should rule the Sudanese. Most of these new men then occupied junior administrative positions; two decades later, however, they were the senior officers who effected a smooth transition from Condominium to independence. Much of their liberalism and tolerance was embodied in an older but remarkable administrator, Sir Douglas Newbold, who joined the political service in 1920. He was appointed civil secretary in 1939 and did much to lay the foundations for a transfer of power from an authoritarian imperial regime to an independent parliamentary democracy which his successor, Sir James Robertson, brilliantly carried out a decade later.

The change in the attitude of the government was accompanied by a growth in the number of educated Sudanese who sought to make their presence felt through the Graduates' General Congress. In the important Anglo-Egyptian treaty of 1936 Britain and Egypt had reached a partial accord which enabled Egyptian officials to return to the Sudan. As in 1924, the Sudanese had not been consulted. The traditional *shaykhs* and chiefs could not have cared less, but the new Sudanese elite were bitterly resentful that neither Britain nor Egypt bothered to solicit their opinions. Thus, they began to express their grievances through the Graduates' General Congress, which had been established in February 1938 as an alumni association of Gordon College and soon embraced all educated Sudanese. At first the Graduates' General Congress confined its interests to social and educational activities, but after the visit of the prime minister of Egypt, Ali Mahir, to the Sudan in 1940 the Egyptians sought to use the Congress against the British by encouraging the organization with financial and moral support to turn increasingly to political action. In 1942 the Congress officially put forth its claims to act as the spokesman for Sudanese nationalism. The Sudan government abruptly refused to consider such a sweeping demand. Hitherto the Sudan government had regarded the Congress with paternal benevolence, but not even the good will of Newbold could welcome the constitutional and political implications of such a claim when the British were desperately fighting the Italians in Ethiopia and the Germans in Egypt. When the Sudan government rejected their claims, the Congress split into two groups: a moderate majority which was prepared to accept the good faith of the government, and an extremist minority led by Ismail al-Azhari which, under the slogan "Unity of the Nile Valley," turned to Egypt. By vigor and demagoguery Azhari soon consolidated his influence throughout the towns and among the educated extremists. By 1943 his supporters had won control of the Congress and organized the Ashiqqa (Brothers), the first genuine political party in the Sudan. Seeing the initiative pass to the extremists, the moderates formed the Umma (Nation) Party, designed to cooperate with the British toward independence under the patronage of Sayyid Abd al-Rahman al-Mahdi, the posthumous son of the Mahdi.

At this point the traditional authoritarianism of Sudanese society emerged to compromise the liberal democracy advocated by the Sudanese elite. Hitherto they had been divorced, and those Sudanese educated in Western political ideas and cultural ways had been adrift from the mass of Sudanese who were content to remain aloof from politics and continue their dependence upon their traditional, authoritarian leaders. Now the new political forces, ideologically strong but numerically weak, called upon the Sudanese masses to redress the balance between the rulers and the ruled. It was a powerful combination with sweeping implications, for traditional Sudanese society in the Northern Sudan was still very much divided between the riverine population, the Awlad al-balad, and the western nomads. By associating themselves with the opposing political programs of the Sudanese elite, they revived ancient religious rivalries and cultural feuds which had temporarily been laid to rest by the imposition of British imperial rule.

On the one hand was Sayyid Abd al-Rahman, the leader of the Ansar, the Mahdists, who had inherited the allegiance of the thousands who had followed his father and who were now prepared to follow the son. A man of consummate ability and shrewdness, Sayyid Abd al-Rahman had supported the British in both great wars and had been suitably rewarded by power and influence. He now sought to combine to his own advantage this power and influence with the ideology of the Umma. On the other was Sayyid Ali

al-Mirghani, the leader of the Khatmiyya brotherhood, the great
religious rival of the Ansar. As Sayyid Abd al-Rahman's fortunes
advanced during the interwar years, those of Sayyid Ali had seemed,
by comparison, to decline. The Khatmiyya had supported the Egyptian administration in the nineteenth century but was eclipsed by
Mahdism, only to be revived in the early years of the Condominium
and nurtured by the British, who sought a counterweight to the
influence of Mahdism. Alarmed by the resurgence of Mahdism,
Sayyid Ali, although he personally remained aloof from politics,
threw his support to Azhari and to Egypt, whose history was so
closely bound up with his own. At the same time Sayyid Abd al-
Rahman identified himself with the Umma and continued to
cooperate with the Sudan government.

Thus the religious and cultural rift among the Northern Sudanese
which had conditioned their past was now deepened by all the
emotional and secular fanaticism of twentieth-century politics. The
competition between the Azhari-Khatmiyya faction, remodeled in
1951 as the National Unionist Party (NUP), and the Umma-Ansar
group quickly rekindled the old suspicions and deep-seated hatreds
to sour Sudanese politics for years and eventually to strangle parliamentary democracy in the Sudan.

Although the Sudan government had crushed the initial hopes of
the Congress, the administration was aware of the pervasive power
of nationalism among the elite and sought to introduce new institutions to associate the Sudanese more closely with the task of governing. Under the leadership of the Governor-General Sir Hubert
Huddleston, who had former experience in the Sudan, and the
guidance of the civil secretary, Sir Douglas Newbold, an advisory
council was established for the Northern Sudan consisting of the
governor-general, his secretaries, and twenty-eight Sudanese. Unfortunately, the advisory council satisfied neither the Sudanese nor the
Egyptians. The Egyptians regarded it as yet another clever British
device to exclude Egyptian participation in the governing of the
Sudan. The Sudanese intelligentsia regarded it as merely a debating
society, for its decisions could not be enforced. Moreover, the council
was made up mostly of tribal elders, whose traditional attitudes
worked to the advantage of an authoritarian administration and
against the liberalism demanded by the elite. Finally, affairs in the
Southern Sudan were excluded from the deliberations of the council,

NASSER'S EGYPT AND INDEPENDENT SUDAN   151

and for the first time in this century the Southern Sudan loomed as a divisive influence.

Until Sudanese and British officials began to ponder the future of the Sudan, the southern provinces had long been ignored by the central government except when troops or money were required. The central administration in Khartoum was dominated by officials whose background and service had been in the Northern Sudan. They had little knowledge and no previous experience of the South and were content to leave those eccentric Bog Barons alone in return for pacification of the South at the lowest possible cost to the Sudanese treasury. Once the Southern Sudan was brought completely under British control in the late 1920s, the central authorities could no longer ignore its administration. They first had to recognize the fundamental differences between the Northern and Southern Sudanese and fashion their policy accordingly. Racially, the North claims to be Arab, the South Negroid. In religion the North is Muslim, the South is pagan and Christian. The North speaks Arabic, the South some eighty different African languages. Once having acknowledged these distinctions, the Sudan government sought to apply the principles of indirect rule which had become so fashionable in the North. But for the government to follow the precepts of indirect rule and "build up a series of self-contained racial and tribal units with structure and organization based, to whatever extent the requirements of equity and good government permit, upon indigenous customs, traditional usage, and beliefs," Southern Sudanese, African participation in the administration and the revitalization of their customs would be necessary, but hardly possible if such customs were continually eroded by contacts with the Arabic-speaking peoples of the Northern Sudan.[2] Consequently, under the direction of Mac-Michael a "Southern policy" was fashioned in 1930 to encourage indigenous growth by eradicating Northern Sudanese, Muslim, Arab influences. For nearly two decades thereafter the Southern Sudan was sealed off from the North and the vestiges of the Arab, Muslim presence gradually rooted out.

Like most administrative decisions the policy of exclusion was not without precedent. Wingate had encouraged Christian missionary work in the Southern Sudan, not so much because he himself was a

[2] Memorandum on Southern Policy, January 25, 1930, by Sir Harold Mac-Michael, Bahr al-Ghazal, I/1/1, Sudan Government Archives.

devout Christian, but because by sending Christian missionaries to the pagan Sudan he could more easily keep them out of the Muslim North and at the same time build a Christian bulwark against the spread of Islam southward up the Nile. Until their expulsion in 1964 Christian missionaries, particularly the Catholic Verona Fathers and the Anglican Church Missionary Society, provided most of the Western education in the Southern Sudan. Although staffed by devoted missionaries and teachers whose influence was widespread, neither the missionary societies nor the government ever had sufficient resources to produce a class of educated elite. Wingate's religious programs had their secular counterpart, and in 1910 he ordered the formation of an Equatorial Corps of Southerners for service in the South, commanded by British officers speaking English and practicing Christianity. Not only did the Equatorial Corps replace the Northern Sudanese garrisons, who had been primarily responsible for spreading Islam and Arabic, but its formation created a non-Muslim, non-Arab reserve for use against any uprising in the North. By 1918 most Northern troops had left the South, and Sunday replaced Friday as the official day of worship. Twelve years later MacMichael's Southern policy extended the exclusion of Northern Sudanese to include not only Arabic-speaking Muslim troops but merchants, teachers, and technicians as well.

To the Northern Sudanese nationalist, the Southern policy appeared to be a typical Machiavellian plot by which the British were to divide and rule and further, a scheme to sever the South from the North to create for the former a different, if not separate, status. The strict silence which the government maintained about Southern affairs only increased the suspicions of the Northerners, who in their ignorance attributed deep, dark designs where none in reality existed. For years Southern policy was one of "the main topics of [well-informed] conversation at effendis' tea parties in Omdurman." [3] When the Northern Sudanese began agitating to transform the advisory council into a legislative one, the policy of exclusion and the future status of the Southern Sudan could no longer be ignored. Was the South to be represented in any future legislative council and thereby irrevocably committed to the Sudan as a whole, or was it to remain outside of the council, developing political maturity until it should be able to take part in the council's deliberations or

[3] "Undated Notes on Southern Policy," by D. J. Bethell, Bahr al-Ghazal, I/1/2, Sudan Government Archives.

even choose different political ties? The question was resolved at a conference of British officials and Northern and Southern Sudanese representatives at Juba in 1947. The Southerners determined to send delegates to a legislative council of a united Sudan, and the Sudan government correspondingly decided to abandon its policy of excluding Northern Sudanese from the South. Thus, just at the time when the pace of Sudanese nationalism quickened, the Southern Sudanese arrived on the political scene, with their largely uneducated, clearly unsophisticated, and predominately tribalized and tradition-oriented societies.

If the Egyptians had regarded the creation of an advisory council with suspicion, they adamantly refused to accept British proposals for a legislative council. As in the past, however, the British paid little heed to Egyptian fulminations and unilaterally forged ahead to meet Sudanese objections by holding elections for a council. These elections were boycotted by Ismail al-Azhari's pro-Egyptian Ashiqqa, giving control of the new Legislative Council to the Umma. The Egyptians reacted with panic as they saw the unity of the Nile Valley slipping from them and in October 1951 unilaterally abrogated the Anglo-Egyptian agreement of 1936 and proclaimed Faruq king of Egypt and the Sudan. These hasty and ill-considered actions only managed to alienate the Sudanese from Egypt. As for the British, they not only refused to recognize the abrogation but went one step further in their courtship of the Sudanese and introduced in 1952 a self-governing statute for the Sudan into the Legislative Council.

The Egyptian government would probably have never agreed to self-government for the Sudan if the old structure of Egyptian politics had not been suddenly swept away by the Nasser-Naguib revolution in Egypt in July 1952. The military men who took control at Cairo were not only more flexible than their predecessors but more understanding of Sudanese aspirations. On the one hand, they sought an accommodation with Britain. On the other, they set out to reestablish Egyptian influence in the Sudan. By 1953 they appeared to have been extraordinarily successful in implementing both policies. On February 12, 1953, the Codomini, Britain and Egypt, signed an agreement granting self-government for the Sudan and self-determination within three years for the Sudanese. The military rulers of Egypt had recognized on their part the realities of Sudanese nationalism, while the British on theirs had accepted certain modifications, all of which were proposed by Egypt to the advantage of the Sudanese and toward the restoration of close ties between the Sudanese political parties and the military regime in Egypt. Elections for a representative parliament to rule the Sudan followed in November and December 1953. The Egyptians threw their support behind Ismail al-Azhari, the leader of the Ashiqqa-Khatmiyya coalition recently recreated as the National Unionist Party, who campaigned on the slogan "Unity of the Nile Valley." This position was opposed by the Umma Party, which had the less vocal but pervasive support of British officials. Led by Sayyid Abd al-Rahman, the Umma campaigned for an independent Sudan. To the shock of many British officials and to the chagrin of the Umma Party, which had enjoyed power in the Legislative Council for nearly six years, Azhari's NUP won an overwhelming victory.

At once Egyptians, British, and many Sudanese interpreted the victory as a mandate for Azhari to fashion some form of association between the Sudan and Egypt. This soon proved to be a grossly misleading interpretation. By voting for the NUP the electors had simply expressed their wish for freedom from British control, not for union with Egypt. Because the Umma had cooperated with the British for so long in the Legislative Council, they were widely regarded as tools of the administration and lacked national support. Many Sudanese were also highly suspicious of the dynastic ambitions of Sayyid Abd al-Rahman. The real meaning of the election soon became apparent to the astute Azhari, and he realized that a large and powerful segment of the Sudanese population, tribesmen and intelligentsia alike, while anxious to end British rule, was also bitterly opposed to union with Egypt. In March 1954 when Naguib visited Khartoum he was greeted by huge protest demonstrations in which several people were killed. Gross Egyptian propaganda and rumors of Egyptian bribery of Sudanese politicians were given credence by the ridiculous behavior of Egyptian government officials visiting the Sudan. Moreover, the Sudanese, having suddenly discovered themselves masters of their fate, were not about to hand over their destiny to Egypt.

This revelation was made clear by the mutiny and rebellion which swept through the Equatoria Province of the Southern Sudan in August 1955. In the preparations for self-government and self-determination the wishes of the South were given little notice. The competent but paternal British administrators left, their places taken by inexperienced and frequently intolerant Northerners. Offended, confused, and misunderstood by Northern politicians, the Southern Sudanese soon erupted, first in a mutiny by the Equatorial Corps, then in disorders and rebellion throughout the province. Nearly three hundred Northern Sudanese were killed before the revolt was suppressed, but the restoration of order was long and difficult. The rebellion had numerous causes, among them the great racial, religious, and linguistic gulf between the Northern and Southern Sudanese, but fundamentally it was a reaction to Northern Arab domination in the administration of the Southern Sudan. Sobered by the realities of discontent and the responsibilities of political power and authority, Ismail al-Azhari disowned his own campaign promises of union with Egypt and declared the Sudan an independent republic on January 1, 1956, to be henceforth guided by an elected representative parliament. The liberalism of the present appeared to have triumphed over the traditional authoritarianism of the past.

The parliamentary government which ruled the Sudan from 1956 to 1958 was an outgrowth of political developments since 1953. Ironically, when Azhari had ceased to support unity with Egypt and sought to lead the movement toward independence, his party, the NUP, lost its ideology and dissolved into factional infighting. Even before his declaration of independence he had lost a vote of confidence in the legislative assembly, and his position was only narrowly restored five days later. Sayyid Ali al-Mirghani and his Khatmiyya were becoming increasingly disenchanted with Azhari, whose personal quarrels with Sayyid Ali's lieutenants were hardly calculated to smooth over political differences. By June 1956 the NUP had split, and Azhari had broken with the Khatmiyya. With the support of Sayyid Ali, who months before had held a dramatic meeting with his rival Sayyid Abd al-Rahman, a dissident faction of the NUP established the Peoples Democratic Party (PDP) and on July 5, 1956, formed a coalition government with the Umma Party in which Azhari was excluded from office. A leading member of the Umma Party, Abd Allah Khalil, was elected prime minister and remained in power until the *coup d'état* of 1958.

The coalition of the Umma Party and the PDP was a cynic's delight. On every issue the two parties had opposite objectives. The Umma Party was friendly to Britain and the West. It wished to see Sayyid Abd al-Rahman al-Mahdi as president of the republic for life. The PDP's policy was oriented toward Egypt, which looked in turn to the Soviet bloc. Obviously, the Peoples Democratic Party could not tolerate the elevation of Sayyid Abd al-Rahman at the expense of Sayyid Ali. The coalition was kept together only by a mutual desire to keep Azhari and the rump of the NUP, which had followed him into opposition, from coming to power. Political stability and respect for parliamentary government cannot be built on such opportunism.

The triumph of liberal democracy in the Sudan was short-lived. Against the strength of tradition, which still shaped the life of the Sudanese, the liberalism imported from the West, disseminated through British education, and adopted by the Sudanese intelligentsia was quickly compromised. At first parliamentary government had been held in high esteem in the Sudan. It was the symbol of nationalism and independence, a pubescent rite which signified the coming of age and freedom from alien rule. But at best parliament was a superficial instrument. It had been introduced into the Sudan at precisely the time when parliamentary forms were rapidly disappearing from other countries in the Middle East. Parties, the machinery by which parliamentary government functions, were not well organized groups with distinct objectives, but loose alliances attached opportunistically to personal interests and sectarian loyalties. Such groups were difficult to manage, almost impossible to direct. When the tactics of party management were exhausted, parliament became debased, benefiting only those politicians who reaped the rewards of power and patronage. Disillusioned with their experiment in liberal democracy, the Sudanese turned once again to the authoritarianism to which their traditions had accustomed them.

On the night of November 16, 1958, the commander-in-chief of the Sudan Army, General Ibrahim Abbud, sent four thousand troops into Omdurman and Khartoum, seized the government buildings and radio station, placed the ministers under house arrest, and took charge of the government in a bloodless *coup d'état*. The following day Abbud himself broadcast to the nation, blaming the "state of degeneration" on the political strife between rival factions. He dissolved all political parties, prohibited assemblies, and temporarily suspended newspapers. The country was henceforth governed by a supreme council of the armed forces, consisting of twelve senior officers. Parliament was abolished, the transitional constitution suspended, and a state of emergency proclaimed. Authoritarian government again controlled the Sudan.

Few in the Sudan mourned the passing of parliament. The mass of Sudanese had regarded the maneuvers of the politicians with bitter cynicism. Indeed, Prime Minister Abd Allah Khalil, himself a retired brigadier, appears to have urged the military takeover to counter the ever-growing Egyptian influence. Even the large political parties did not oppose the *coup*. The leading politicians were pensioned off and in fact seemed relieved to be rid of the task of governing in which they had so lamentably failed. Both the great religious leaders, Sayyid Ali al-Mirghani and Sayyid Abd al-Rahman, welcomed the army's seizure of power. Sayyid Ali could now retire from politics, which he had never liked, and on March 24, 1959, Sayyid Abd al-Rahman died, depriving his followers of their leader. Only the communists opposed the military regime. First organized in 1944 among Sudanese students in Cairo, the Communist Party was a small but well disciplined group which sought support among the students and the powerful trade union movement, particularly the Railway Workers' Union and the Sudan Workers' Trade Union Federation. Under Abbud the Communists were dealt with severely.

Although the country as a whole accepted military dictatorship, the army did not. During the first year of army rule factions and personalities within the army struggled for control of the supreme council. Abbud himself seemed above all this. A fatherly figure, whose gentle demeanor and courtly manners impressed foreigners and charmed the Sudanese, he remained passive and quiescent. He preferred to act as Head of State and leave the real power to the younger generals who were vying for control of the council. At first the council was dominated by Major General Ahmad Abd al-Wahhab, second in command of the army, but in March 1959 he was challenged by two brigadiers, Muhyi al-Din Ahmad Abd Allah and Abd al-Rahim Shannan. On March 9 the two conspirators brought troops to Khartoum, momentarily gained control of the council, and in May forced the retirement of Abd al-Wahhab. Muhyi al-Din and Shannan, however, did not secure their positions. They and their supporters were still a minority on the council, and before the end of June the two brigadiers were arrested, accused of inciting mutiny, openly tried, and sentenced to life imprisonment. Several other officers were dismissed from the army and others demoted. One other attempted coup took place in November when a young officer led a revolt in the infantry school at Omdurman. The rising was quickly suppressed, and within a week the ringleaders were tried and executed. The executions sobered the Sudanese, who had hitherto been proud of the bloodless means by which the Abbud government had seized and maintained power. His regime was never again threatened by the army.

Despite these internal struggles, army rule brought rapid improvement in the Sudan's deteriorating economic position. The parliamentary government had always insisted on selling the cotton crop at a fixed price. Thus, when cotton prices slumped on the world market in 1958, Sudan cotton went unsold at its unrealistic high price. Nearly 250,000 bales remained from the 1958 crop, with a second bumper harvest expected in 1959. The Abbud government at once abolished the fixed price and within six months had sold all the Sudanese cotton. Although disposed of at lower rates, the ultimate effect of the cotton sale was to give the Sudan a surplus revenue and dramatically rebuild the nation's foreign reserves. The other achievement of the military government was the conclusion of a Nile waters agreement with the United Arab Republic. The governments resumed in October 1959 the discussions the parliamentary regime had broken off in acrimony over a year before. Within one month agreement was reached, and a Nile waters treaty was signed on November 8, 1959. The Sudan received £E15 million compensation for the land at Wadi Halfa to be flooded by the Aswan Dam, and a reapportionment of the water was agreed upon, thereby paving the way for the construction of the Roseires Dam near the Ethiopian frontier to provide stored water for further large-scale irrigation projects in the Sudan. Although both the monetary compensation and the Sudan's share of the water have proven insufficient, the Nile waters agreement was more significant than the inadequate technical division implies, for the United Arab Republic not only recognized but appeared to be reconciled to an independent Sudan on her southern frontier astride the water upon which Egypt depends.

These were positive achievements, and the military government capitalized on the improvements in the economy and relations with Egypt to enhance its international prestige and consolidate its internal position. By 1960 the military regime appeared secure. The threat of a counterrevolution had disappeared, and the Sudan would have appeared a model of authoritarian, progressive government if not for the problem of the Southern Sudan. During the short-lived parliamentary government the politicians seem to have had no coherent policy for the South except to win the votes of Southern representatives first by promises and then by threats. Neither was effective, and when the Equatoria Province erupted into rebellion in 1955, the principal object of the government was simply to maintain its control in the region and preserve a united Sudan.

The determination by Northern Sudanese to continue the union of the two disparate regions was rooted in Sudanese nationalism, wherein all the strength of Arab language, Arab culture, and the Arab past were fused with the powerful traditions of Sudanese tribal history and the deep emotions of Sudanese Islam. Built on the skeleton of British imperial rule, nationalism in the Sudan was the dominate, unifying force in this vast and diverse land. Thus, when Sudanese leaders called upon the forces of nationalism to unify the country, they appealed to ideas and passions primarily associated with Arabization and Islamization. These are strong and effective themes in the Northern Sudan. They have little relevance in the South. But the multiplicity of weak, local cultures in the South could hardly withstand the more powerful and vigorous culture of the North. In effect, the paramountcy of indigenous cultures in the southern provinces and the primary concern for their growth in an African environment died with the abandonment of Southern policy in 1947. If Sudanese nationalism was to remain a viable ideology for the preservation of a united Sudan, the indigenous customs of the South would inevitably be challenged by the Arab, Muslim practices of the North. Partly in fear of another rebellion and partly restricted by the moderation imposed upon them under a parliamentary system, the politicians failed to press Arabization and Islamization in the South. The army officers of the military government were under no such restraints. They increasingly employed Arabization and Islamization in the name of Sudan unity and saw no contradiction in binding the manifold diversities of the Sudan with the cords of Sudanese nationalism. In the South the Abbud regime introduced numerous measures designed to facilitate the spread of Arabic and Islam. Important positions in the administration and police were staffed by Northerners. The Southern Liberal Party, which represented the views of the core of Southern intellectuals, was proscribed. Education was shifted from the English curriculum of the Christian missionaries, who had long been solely responsible for education in the South, to an Arabic, Islamic orientation. Islam was proselytized by the construction of mosques, the spread of propaganda, and the establishment of Islamic schools, all under the direction of the department of religious affairs. Foreign Christian missionaries were increasingly restricted and finally expelled in February and March 1964. The missionaries left behind immature Sudanese Christian churches to struggle for self-preservation against the growing strength of Islam backed by the power and resources of the Sudan government.

The Southerners' reaction to these political and religious pressures and the economic and educational neglect was flight and rebellion. Ever since the disturbances in 1955 the Southern Sudanese had fled to Uganda and the Congo, particularly members of border tribes whose kinsmen lived across the frontier. The flow of refugees then decreased to a trickle during the dying days of parliamentary government in the Sudan. The military seizure of the government did not at first precipitate a fresh flight or new outbreak of disturbances, but after 1960 when the military government began pressing Arabization and Islamization on the South, the trickle again became a flood. Many Southern intellectuals and members of the Southern Liberal Party who had not been associated with the disorders in 1955 now fled to establish in exile the Sudan African National Union (SANU) to present the Southern point of view and to work peacefully, if with futility, for the old demand of the Southern Liberal Party for a federated Sudan. The tribesmen were simply herded into refugee camps by the harried and somewhat embarrassed government officials of the Congo and Uganda.

In the Southern Sudan itself the measures of the central government were greeted by ever-increasing resistance. In October 1962 a widespread strike in Southern schools resulted in antigovernment demonstrations followed by a general flight of students and others over the border. During the spring and summer of 1963 feelings relaxed and affairs appeared to improve, most of the discontented having fled, and the Sudan government reinforced its army and police units in the southern provinces. Suddenly, however, in September 1963 rebellion again erupted in eastern Equatoria and in the Upper Nile Province led by the Anya Nya, a Southern Sudanese terrorist organization. Bitterly opposed to the policies of the government, and disenchanted with the ineffectual attempts by the leaders of the Sudan African National Union to reach a settlement, the Anya Nya declared open hostility toward the Northern Sudanese in the South in the belief that only violent resistance would make the government of General Abbud seek a solution acceptable to the

Southerners. Taking refuge in the illimitable bush, the terrorists continued their sporadic attacks on isolated posts of the Sudan army, while the Southern Sudanese carried on their way of life much as before, wandering off when the pressure of government became too great, returning when the weight of administration relaxed. Without confidence, however, there was little growth or progress in any field. Thus, while economic and educational developments transformed the North, the South remained a stagnant backwater in a rapidly developing world. Blind to the aspirations of the Southern Sudanese and devoid of imagination in their dealings with them, the generals in Khartoum sought to establish their authority by repression which increased in proportion to Southern discontent. To prevent the flow of refugees, the Sudan signed extradition treaties in March 1964 with Ethiopia and Uganda, but these measures had little effect in the wilds of the frontiers.

Unable to recover internal security in the southern provinces, the Sudan government announced in September 1964 that a twenty-five man commission would investigate conditions in the Southern Sudan. The formation of such a commission was itself a confession of the government's failure to acquire control or to restore confidence, and with every passing month the magnitude of this failure became increasingly apparent to the Northern Sudanese and even to the world beyond. Although the Northern Sudanese had little sympathy for their countrymen in the South, the intelligentsia were able to use the government's failure there to assail authoritarian rule in the North and to revive demands for democratic government which the military *coup d'état* had brought to an abrupt end.

The Northern Sudanese had at first welcomed General Abbud's government and then passively accepted it. By 1962, however, numerous urban elements, including the intelligentsia, the trade unions, and the civil servants, as well as the powerful religious brotherhoods, were bored and disgusted with the military regime. In 1958 these groups had applauded the efforts of the patriotic and progressive army officers to clean the Augean stables of Sudanese parliamentarianism and to solve pressing economic and international problems. But within a few years, after the military government had consolidated its power, the intelligentsia resented its exclusion from the councils of government, the trade unions chafed at the restrictions placed upon their activities, and the civil servants sulked at orders from their military ministers. Even the more conservative religious brotherhoods grew restless when they were unable to carry on their former political activities. Moreover, the tribal masses and growing proletariat had become increasingly apathetic toward the government, for even if the parliamentarians were corrupt, they were at least exciting. Military reviews, parades, and heroic pronouncements were no substitute for the enthusiasm of party politics and the passions stirred by political action. Even if they considered the problem, the military rulers never provided an outlet for the political frustrations of the Sudanese, and in the end the regime was overwhelmed by boredom and overthrown by the reaction to its lassitude. The means of its overthrow, not the cause, was the Southern Sudan.

Following the establishment of the commission of enquiry in September 1964, students at Khartoum University created their own discussion groups to express their dissatisfaction with the government's policies in the South. On October 22, 1964, the students held a meeting in defiance of a government prohibition in order to condemn publicly these policies and to denounce the regime. In the ensuing and inevitable clash with the police, one student was killed and several were wounded. Larger demonstrations followed in Khartoum, Omderman, and Khartoum North, and with most of its forces committed in the Southern Sudan, the military regime was unable to maintain control in the three cities. The disorders soon spread to other towns along the Nile and into the interior. Unable to govern without civilian support, and unwilling to crush the disturbances with massive repression, General Abbud first announced the dismissal of the supreme council and a few days later the end of the military government itself. Abbud resigned shortly thereafter as Head of State and a transitional government was appointed to take the place of the military rulers and to govern under the provisional constitution of 1956.

Under the leadership of Sirr al-Khatim al-Khalifa, the provisional government faced two difficult tasks: to regain the confidence of the Southern Sudanese in the administration, and to transfer power to an elected, representative government. The Southern problem was the most critical, for in December rioting between Northern and Southern Sudanese erupted in Khartoum, lasting for several days and leaving numerous killed and hundreds wounded before order was restored. Seeking to resolve the gulf of misunderstanding and animosity, the provisional government sent a delegation to Uganda to negotiate an amnesty with Southern leaders and to arrange a conference to discuss the Southern problem. Although originally scheduled to meet at Juba in February 1965, the failure to institute a cease fire with the Anya Nya terrorists delayed the opening until March and required that the site be moved to Khartoum. Here all the principle political groups from the North and the South as well as observers from various African states gathered and in a week of frank exchange of widely divergent points of view demonstrated not only the differences between North and South but the conflicts among the Southerners themselves. Some Southerners demanded autonomy within the Sudan, others separation from it. The Northerners insisted upon national unity, although they were willing to accept some devolution of power. Despite the intransigence of both groups, the conference was held together by the efforts of the observing African states and resolved to send a peace commission to the South to try to reestablish order and administration. In the meantime, the provisional government turned to its second task—elections in the Northern Sudan to determine the composition of a representative government.

The elections were held in April and May 1965. The Umma Party won seventy-four of the 156 seats contested, followed by the NUP with forty-seven. A leading Umma politician, Muhammad Ahmad Mahjub, who had served as the first foreign minister of the independent Sudan, became prime minister in a coalition government with the NUP, but the early hopes of cooperation with the Southerners have since vanished before Northern intransigence on the one hand and Southern indecision, disunity, and paucity of leadership on the other. The Northern Sudanese have remained firm, stubbornly refusing to concede the Southern demand for federation. The Southern Sudanese have remained distrustful of the Arabs and intractable in their demands. As the political deadlock deepens, the attempts to resolve it by force have been escalated. Many Southerners have been killed, others continue to flee into exile, but the Sudan army has suffered many casualties inflicted by Southern guerrillas and in fact controls only the towns. Beyond, in the countryside, there is no civil administration, no health services, no food distribution; the Southern Sudan is deteriorating into a quiet, verdant wasteland.

Nevertheless, despite the failure to resolve the Southern problem, parliamentary government has returned to the Sudan, and once again the Sudanese elite have set out to establish a conservative democracy. Their success, however, will be conditioned as much by their own ability to make parliamentary government work as by their ability to deal with the two great issues before a democratic Sudan: the containment of authoritarian forces, which remain strong and powerful throughout the country, and the reconciliation of Southern demands with Sudanese nationalism.

Unlike most non-Western countries Egypt and the Sudan
have been blessed with a number of excellent historical studies in English or French which are reasonably accessible to anyone wishing to
pursue the histories of Egypt and the Sudan in greater detail. Should the
reader decide to delve even more deeply into any particular subject, he
can find comprehensive bibliographies in most of the books mentioned
in this essay.

Any analysis of Egypt must start with the Nile, and any attempt to
study the Nile should begin with Harold E. Hurst's *The Nile: A General
Account of the River and the Utilization of Its Waters* (London: Con-
stable & Co., Ltd., 1952). This book, written by an engineer who worked
a lifetime on Nile irrigation projects, gives a comprehensive picture of the
river and man's efforts to control its waters for cultivation. The social
setting of Egyptian life can be studied in numerous works. Edward Lane,
An Account of the Manners and Customs of the Modern Egyptians, 2
vols. (London: 1836), was written by a European orientalist before the
full impact of modernization had begun to transform Egyptian society,
and it gives an excellent picture of the traditional society. J. Lozach and
G. Hug, *L'Habitat Rural en Égypte* (Cairo: 1930) portray the rural
society and the vast changes wrought by hydraulic developments. Hamad
Ammar's *Growing Up in an Egyptian Village: Silwa, Province of Aswan*
(London: 1954) is the only full-scale and rigorous sociological analysis of
an Egyptian village community, a model of social research. Its findings
can be supplemented by reading Egyptian novels, several of which, by
Taha Hysayn and Tawfiq al-Hakim, have been translated into English.
An attempt has been made to discuss the personality type of the Arabs
by Sania Hamady, *Temperament and Character of the Arabs* (New
York: 1960). There is certainly a great deal to quibble with in this work,
but the generalizations are always interesting and stimulate further
research. Egypt's growing population can be studied in almost all of the
works on modern Egypt. The most reliable guide to statistics of this type

is Charles Issawi, *Egypt in Revolution* (New York: 1963). On urbanization there is an article by Janet Abu-Lughod, "Urbanization in Egypt: Present State and Future Prospects," *Economic Development and Cultural Change*, XIII, No. 3 (April 1965), 313-43.

There are a host of general works which will introduce the reader to the history of ancient Egypt, a subject which this book does not cover. They include James H. Breasted, A *History of Egypt* (New York: 1959); W. B. Emery, *Archaic Egypt* (Baltimore: 1961), and Margaret A. Murray, *The Splendor That Was Egypt*, 2nd ed., (New York: 1963).

In dealing with the pre-modern Islamic history of Egypt, one naturally turns to the standard histories of the area: Philip Hitti, *History of the Arabs* (London: 1950), Carl Brockelmann, *History of the Islamic Empire* (New York: 1942), Bernard Lewis, *The Arabs in History* (London: 1950), and George Kirk, A *Short History of the Middle East* (London: 1948). Probably the best short introduction to Islamic institutions is H. A. R. Gibb, *Mohammedanism* (New York: 1953). For Egypt in particular there are also some general histories: Stanley Lane-Poole, A *History of Egypt* (New York: 1901), Gaston Wiet, *L'Egypte Arabe de la Conquête Arabe à la Conquête Ottomane, 642-1517* (Paris: 1937), and Henri Dehérain, *L'Egypte Turque: Pachas et Mameluks du XVIe au XVIIIe Siècle: L'Expédition du Général Bonaparte* (Paris: 1931).

Many works treat the life of Muhammad; the two volumes by Montgomery Watt, *Muhammad at Mecca* (Oxford: 1953) and *Muhammad at Medina* (Oxford: 1956) incorporate the latest findings of scholars on the subject.

If the student wishes to pursue pre-modern Egyptian history further, it is necessary to consult articles in scholarly journals. Jean Sauvaget's *Introduction à l'Histoire de l'Orient Musulman; Elements de Bibliographie* (Paris: 1961), an excellent general bibliographical guide, includes references to the most important periodical literature. On the conquest and early administration of Egypt there is Emile Amelineau, "La Conquête de l'Egypte par les Arabes," *Revue Historique*, CXIX (1915), 273-310 and CXX (1915), 1-25; H. I. Bell, "The Administration of Egypt under the Umayyad Khalifs," *Byzantinische Zeitschrift*, XXVIII (1928), 278-86; and Henri Lammens, "Un Gouveneur Omayyade d'Egypte, Qorra ibn Sarik, d'Après les Papyrus Arabes," *Etudes sur le Siècle des Omayyades* (Beirut: 1930), 305-23. Still the most important general study of this period is Wellhausen's *The Arab Kingdom and Its Fall* (Calcultta: 1927).

The Abbasid revolution has been traced in Bernard Lewis' article on the Abbasids in the *Encyclopedia of Islam*. Zaky Mohamed Hassan has written a full length study of the Tulunids: *Les Tulunids: Etude de l'Egypte Musulmane à la Fin du IXe Siècle, 868-905* (Paris: 1933). On the Fatimids one should consult Bernard Lewis, *The Origins of Ismailism* (Cambridge: 1940), W. Ivanow, *The Rise of the Fatimids* (London: 1942), DeLacy O'Leary, *A Short History of the Fatimid Caliphate* (London: 1923), P. J. Vatikiotis, *The Fatimid Theory of State* (Lahore: 1957), and his "The Rise of Extremist Sects and the Dissolution of the Fatimid Empire in Egypt," *Islamic Culture*, XXXI, No. 1 (1957), 17-26. The articles by Claude Cahen entitled "L'Evolution Sociale du Monde Musulman jusqu'au XIIe Siècle face à celle du Monde Chrétien," *Cahiers de Civilisation Médiévale*, I (1958), 451-63, and II (1959), 37-51, are very suggestive and stimulating. They try to make some significant generalizations about the main features of Islamic civilization in comparison with medieval Europe and the Byzantine empire.

For the Mamluk period of Egyptian history the work of one scholar dominates. All of David Ayalon's (David Neustadt) writings are worth serious study. These include "The System of Payment in Mamluk Military Society," *Journal of the Economic and Social History of the Orient*, I, (1957), 37-65 and 257-96; "The Circassians in the Mamluk Kingdom," *Journal of the American Oriental Society*, LXIX (1949), 135-47; "The Wafdiyah in the Mamluk Kingdom," *Islamic Culture*, XXV (1951), 89-104; "Studies on the Structure of the Mamluk Army," *Bulletin of the School of Oriental and African Studies*, XV (1953), 203-228, 448-76, and XVI (1954), 57-90; *Gunpowder and Firearms in the Mamluk Kingdom* (London: 1956); and *L'Esclavage du Mamelouk* (Jerusalem: 1951). The very considerable development of external trade in this and preeeding periods has been studied in S. D. Goitein, "The Rise of the Near Eastern Bourgeoisie in Early Islamic Times," *Journal of World History*, III, No. 3 (1957), 583-604, and "New Light on the Beginnings of the Karim Merchants," *Journal of the Economic and Social History of the Orient*, I (1958), 175-84; Walter J. Fischel, "The Spice Trade in Mamluk Egypt," *Journal of the Economic and Social History of the Orient*, I (1958), 157-74; and E. Ashtor, "The Karimi Merchants," *Journal of the Royal Asiatic Society*, I (1956), 45-56. A. N. Poliak, "Les Revoltes Populaires en Egypte à l'Epoque des Mamelouks et leurs Causes Economiques," *Reveue des Etudes Islamiques*, VIII (1934), 251-73, is an excellent study of this important subject.

The Ottoman period has had the least serious study. For the latter half of the eighteenth century the best introduction to institutions and history is still the work of the French scholars taken by Napoleon to Egypt: *Description de l'Egypte: Etat Moderne*, 4 vols. (Paris: 1809-22). Gibb and Bowen, *Islamic Society and the West*, 2 vols. (London: 1951-57), is a good general work but does not have a great deal of detailed information on Egypt. The best analyses are those of P. M. Holt, "The Career of Kucuk Muhammad (1676-94)," *Bulletin of the School of*

Oriental and African Studies, XXVI (1963), 269-87, and "The Beylicate in Ottoman Egypt During the Seventeenth Century," in the same Journal, XXIV (1961), 214-48. These should be supplemented by Stanford Shaw's *The Financial and Administrative Organization and Development of Ottoman Egypt, 1517-1798* (Princeton: 1962) and *The Ottoman Empire in the Eighteenth Century* (Cambridge: 1962).

Nineteenth-century modernization has begun to receive the attention it deserves. We are, however, much better informed about Muhammad Ali than Ismail. In fact, for the reign of Muhammad Ali there is a general biography, Henry Dodwell, *The Founder of Modern Egypt* (Cambridge: 1931); an analysis of agricultural modernization, Helen A. B. Rivlin, *The Agricultural Policy of Muhammad Ali in Egypt* (Cambridge: 1961); two works on education and translations, J. Heyworth-Dunne, *An Introduction to the History of Education in Modern Egypt* (London: 1939) and Jamal al-Din al-Shayyal, *Al-Tarjamah wa Harakah al-Thaqafah fi Asr Muhammad Ali* (Translations and Cultural Developments in the Reign of Muhammad Ali), (Cairo: 1951); and a general study of reform programs, Gabriel Guermard, *Les Reformes en Egypte* (Cairo: 1936). A. E. Crouchley, *The Economic Development of Modern Egypt* (New York: 1938) is a good economic history of the country.

Unfortunately this volume of high-level scholarship is not available for Ismail's reign. The best work on the period is David Landes, *Bankers and Pashas: International Finance and Economic Imperialism in Egypt* (Cambridge: 1958). Angelo Sammarco, *Histoire de l'Egypte Moderne* (Cairo: 1937) is the only one-volume work in a European language that deserves further mention. For the Suez Canal there is Arnold Wilson, *The Suez Canal* (New York: 1939), and John Marlowe, *The Making of the Suez Canal* (New York: 1964). This period was one of considerable intellectual ferment for Egypt. Much of the writing on Egyptian intellectuals revolves around Muhammad Abduh. The best introduction to Abduh and the men he influenced is Charles C. Adams, *Islam and Modernism in Egypt* (London: 1933). Other good surveys of the intellectual history of Egypt are Nadav Safran, *Egypt in Search of Political Community* (Cambridge: 1961), Albert Hourani, *Arabic Thought in the Liberal Age, 1798-1939* (New York: 1962), Sylvia Haim, *Arab Nationalism* (Berkeley: 1962); and Ibrahim Abu-Lughod, *Arab Rediscovery of Europe* (Princeton: 1963).

The period of British influence in Egypt is rather poorly researched. Abd al-Rahman al-Rafii's study of the Arabi revolt (in Arabic) is probably the most comprehensive treatment of this subject, although marked by strong nationalist biases. Sections of Jacob M. Landau, *Parliaments and Parties in Egypt* (New York: 1954) are very good on the Arabi revolt. Unquestionably, Ronald Robinson and John Gallagher have written the most important recent work on British imperialism in Africa: *Africa and the Victorians: The Official Mind of Imperialism* (New York: 1961), in which Egypt is thoroughly treated. For the British occupation of Egypt the student must still follow the writings of British officials themselves for want of more dispassionate analyses. The best are Lord Cromer, *Modern Egypt*, 2 vols. (London: 1908), Lord Milner, *England in Egypt* (London: 1893), and Auckland Colvin, *The Making of Modern Egypt* (London: 1906). A corrective to these glowing accounts can be found in Abd al-Rahman al-Rafii's biographies (in Arabic) of nationalist leaders Mustafa Kamil and Muhammad Farid. The World War I years which jolted Anglo-Egyptian relations are well treated in P. G. Elgood's critical *Egypt and the Army* (Oxford: 1924). Abd al-Rahman al-Rafii, who is always excellent when treating nationalist outbursts, has written a good study of the postwar Egyptian revolution, *Thawrah Sanah 1919* (The Revolution of 1919) 2 vols., (Cairo: 1946). A more debunking approach is Elie Kedourie, "Sad Zaghlul and the British," *St Antony's Papers* (London: 1961), XI, 139-61.

The interwar period is a great abyss for the historian. One good study by Marcel Colombe, *L'Evolution de l'Egypte, 1924-50* (Paris: 1951), provides some guidelines. Some useful analyses of the Muslim Brotherhood are J. Heyworth-Dunne, *Religious and Political Trends in Modern Egypt* (Washington, D.C.: 1950), Ishak Musa Husaini, *The Moslem Brethren* (Beirut: 1956), and Christina Phelps Harris, *Nationalism and Revolution in Egypt: The Role of the Muslim Brotherhood* (London: 1964). Walter Z. Laqueur, *Communism and Nationalism in the Middle East* (New York: 1956) treats this important subject. Finally, there are two surveys of the war and post-war period by George Kirk: *The Middle East in the War* (New York: 1953), and *The Middle East, 1945-1950* (New York: 1954). But these works hardly scratch the surface of an extremely important period in modern Egyptian history.

The Nasser regime does not lack interpreters. The interested reader should probably start with the works by Egyptians themselves. There are three important ones by participants in the revolution: Gamal Abdel Nasser, *Egypt's Liberation, The Philosophy of Revolution* (Washington, D.C.: 1955), Muhammad Neguib, *Egypt's Destiny: A Personal Statement* (London: 1955), and Anwar al-Sadat, *Revolt on the Nile* (London: 1957). A critical and extremely provocative left-wing account has been written by Anouar Abdel-Malik, *Egypte: Société Militaire* (Paris: 1962). Of the plethora of works in Arabic the best is, once again, Abd al-Rahman al-Rafii, *Thawrah 23 Yuliah, 1952* (The Revolution of July 23, 1952), (Cairo: 1959). There are also numerous Western analyses of the new regime. The two best are P. J. Vatikiotis, *The Egyptian Army in Politics* (Bloomington, Ind.: 1961), and Jean and Simone

Lacouture, *Egypt in Transition* (New York: 1958). These can be supplemented by Tom Little, *Egypt* (London: 1958), Keith Wheelock, *Nasser's New Egypt* (New York: 1960), and Wilton Wynn, *Nasser of Egypt, The Search for Dignity* (Cambridge: 1959). A great deal has been written on the foreign relations of Nasser's Egypt, and most of it tends to be misleading. The most sensible expositions are John C. Campbell, *Defense of the Middle East* (New York: 1960), and John Marlowe, *Arab Nationalism and British Imperialism* (New York: 1961). Finally, no one should overlook two studies of Egyptian economic development: Charles Issawi, *Egypt in Revolution* (New York: 1963), and Doreen Warriner, *Land Reform and Development in the Middle East* (New York: 1962).

Like Egypt, the Sudan has numerous excellent sources in English and even more in the way of comprehensive bibliographies. First and foremost is R. L. Hill, *A Bibliography of the Anglo-Egyptian Sudan From the Earliest Times to 1937* (London: 1939), and its sequel, Abdel Rahman el-Nasri, *A Bibliography of the Sudan 1938-1958* (London: 1962). For literature concerning the Sudan since 1958, *Sudan Notes and Records* publishes reviews and book and periodical lists of the latest materials as well as excellent scholarly articles on specialized subjects pertaining to the Sudan. R. L. Hill has also compiled *A Biographical Dictionary of the Anglo-Egyptian Sudan,* rev. ed. (Oxford: 1966), an indispensible guide to the men who have made the history of the Sudan.

The early history of the Sudan is most adequately presented by Dr. A. J. Arkell, *History of the Sudan From the Earliest Times to 1821,* 2nd ed. (London: 1961). His views are controversial and stimulating, but his later chapters on the coming of the Arabs and Islam need to be supplemented by the first volume of Sir Harold MacMichael, *A History of the Arabs in the Sudan* (Cambridge: 1922). The second volume contains translations of the principal manuscript from which his history has been written. The age of the Funj is most comprehensively covered by O. G. S. Crawford, *The Fung Kingdom of Sennar* (Gloucester: 1951), supported by Andrew Paul, *History of the Beja Tribes of the Sudan* (Cambridge: 1954). For the most recent and sensible discussion of Funj origins the reader should consult P. M. Holt, "Funj Origins: A Critique and New Evidence," *Journal of African History,* IV, No. 1 (1963).

The best recent history of the Sudan from the Funj sultanate to the present is P. M. Holt, *A Modern History of the Sudan* (New York: 1961), which is admirably suited to the general reader. Holt's account can be supplemented by the more specialized studies of the Turkiya, particularly R. L. Hill, *Egypt in the Sudan 1820-1881* (London: 1958), and G. Douin, *Histoire du Règne du Khedive Ismail,* 3 vols. (Cairo: 1933-41). The Mahdist period is brilliantly analyzed by P. M. Holt, *The*

Mahdist State in the Sudan 1881-1898 (Oxford: 1958), but for a more general introduction A. B. Theobald, *The Mahdīya,* (London: 1955), written principally from English sources, provides a readable narrative of the military campaigns.

The reconquest of the Sudan resulted in a great outpouring of historical literature. The campaigns themselves are brilliantly narrated by Winston S. Churchill, *The River War,* 2 vols. (London: 1899). The formulation of British policy which led to the Anglo-Egyptian reconquest is adequately analyzed by Mekki Shibeika, *British Policy in the Sudan, 1882-1902* (London: 1952), and by G. N. Sanderson, *England, Europe, and the Upper Nile, 1882-1899* (Edinburgh: 1965), containing the most recent scholarship and interpretations.

There is no adequate single history of the Anglo-Egyptian Condominium, although Sir Harold MacMichael, *The Sudan* (London: 1954), and J. S. R. Duncan, *The Sudan* (Edinburgh: 1952), and *The Sudan's Path to Independence* (Edinburgh: 1957), present a general survey. Thus the student must seek the story of Anglo-Egyptian rule in a host of biographies, memoirs, and personal reminiscences. The early years of the Condominium can best be seen through the biographies of Wingate, Slatin, and Ali Dinar: Ronald Wingate, *Wingate of the Sudan* (London: 1955), R. L. Hill, *Slatin Pasha* (London: 1964), and A. B. Theobald, *'Alī Dīnār: Last Sultan of Darfur, 1898-1916* (London: 1965). The later history of the Condominium can be extracted from the writings of Douglas Newbold, civil secretary from 1939 to 1945, in *The Making of the Modern Sudan,* ed. K. D. D. Henderson (London: 1953), and Mekki Abbas, *The Sudan Question* (London: 1952). The transitional period of self-government and the vicissitudes of independence have been narrated by K. D. D. Henderson, *Sudan Republic* (London: 1965).

The Southern Sudan has its own historical literature, the most useful being Richard Gray, *History of the Southern Sudan, 1835-1889* (London: 1961), Robert Collins, *The Southern Sudan, 1883-1898* (New Haven: 1962), and J. Oduho and W. Deng, *The Problem of the Southern Sudan* (London: 1963). In addition, there are numerous specialized studies, the most important of which are Arthur Gaitskell, *Gezira* (London: 1959), the account of the Gezira Scheme; K. M. Barbour, *The Republic of the Sudan* (London: 1961), the best comprehensive geography; Saad ed Din Fawzi, *The Labour Movement in the Sudan, 1946-55* (London: 1957), H. C. Squires, *The Sudan Medical Service* (London: 1958), and J. Spencer Trimingham, *Islam in the Sudan* (London: 1949), the best account of traditional Islamic culture in the Sudan.

INDEX

The Modern Nations in Historical Perspective Series